GOODBYE, PERT BREASTS
the diary of a newborn dad

by

Ben Wakeling

For Jessica, Isaac
and the one in the oven

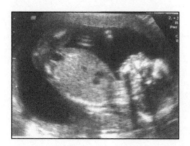

CONTENTS

FOREWORD

I read somewhere in the nether regions of the internet that the first known contraceptive was cow's dung, employed by the Egyptians back in 2000BC. I'm thinking that's probably got to be the most effective contraception *ever*. I have no idea how it was used, where it was slathered, or how it worked, but I do know one thing: if my wife had been clutching a handful of cow poo on that night back in August, there's no way she'd be pregnant right now.

Anyway, I have a confession to make: I'm not actually a newborn dad myself. I already have a two year-old son, Isaac, and so have been through the whole pregnancy thing before. However, each time is different – or so I'm told – and I can remember that on the many, many, *many* excruciating times we trawled around baby shops during our first pregnancy, lapping up impulse buys that have since gathered dust in the loft, there was not one book on the shelves that was aimed purely at the father. They were all like 'Hey, you're going to get hormonal, but that's fine' and 'Don't worry if you poo during labour, it's normal', but there was nothing about what I should expect, and what I could do to help. So I decided to write one myself.

Being a man yourself, you'll undoubtedly have male friends who, when you tell them that you're about to be a father, will roll their eyes, suck in breath and tell you that your life is over. And yes, having a child does restrict freedom, and being a father can be stressful, exasperating and demanding; but all of that stuff is massively outweighed by the pros of having a kid. You never truly realise how much you can love someone until you have a child, and there is nothing as good as watching them grow up, or hear them call you 'Daddy' for the first time. It changes you. You'll become much more sensitive, but you'll also be a bit more resilient. When your kid pukes on your face or poos on your arm, you won't freak out; you'll just wipe it off and carry on. How many of your mates down the pub can say they'll react like that?

In short, then, fatherhood is great. However, I assume that in buying this book you are just at the start of your girlfriend/wife's pregnancy, and thoroughly looking forward to the hormones, morning sickness and bizarre cravings. There's a long way to go yet, but it's worth it, and I hope this book helps you out along the way.

Ben Wakeling

PS. A lot of the images in this book, apart from the cartoon centrefold (which I had commissioned especially for your enjoyment) have been taken from the internet in good faith. If an image is yours, and you're angry, I'm sorry.

PPS. Oh, and one more thing: if your mrs decides to use a breast pump, run like hell. It takes all the joy out of boobies.

WEEK ONE

Or is it Week 4? I can never get my head around this - and I don't think anyone really understands it, even the people who made it up. My wife has tried to explain it to me; it's something to do with the first day of her last period, or the last day of her first period, or something. (You can see how this book is going to help you.) All the internet sites to do with pregnancy seem to term Week One as Week Four, Week Four being the time you actually find out you're pregnant. So, for the sake of scientific accuracy...

WEEK FOUR

A stick, some urine, and a little blue cross

Glad we cleared that up.

It was the 15th August when my wife, Jess, came up to me and announced she was pregnant. We'd been trying for a baby for eight months with no luck, and had almost come to expect that the little reading on the pregnancy test would be negative – so this news came as a big surprise.

I just want to stop here for a minute. The expression 'we're trying for a baby' is one of the most repulsive phrases in the English language. Why? Because as soon as someone says it to you, or you say it to someone else, it immediately conjures up a vivid mental image of the two people in question...y'know. To illustrate my point, choose two of the ugliest people that you know, one man, one woman. They don't even have to be a couple in real life, they just happen to be the most facially challenged people to ever grace your existence. Now, turn to your mrs and say '_____ and _____ are trying for a baby', and watch her face screw up into a picture of grotesqueness as she pictures the two unfortunate beings locked mortal combat. You can try it with anyone, or anything. Big Bird and Miss Piggy are trying for a baby. Disgusting, isn't it? Or comical, whichever way you look at it. Either way, I hope they don't show it on TV to kids.

Anyway, back to the matter in hand. A lot of wives/girlfriends will think of some elaborate way to tell their partners that they're pregnant: leaving the test lying under their pillow, perhaps waiting until they're half asleep - maybe even vomiting morning sickness chunks over their porridge, prompting inevitable questions. Not in this case. I was in the kitchen – making yet another cup of tea – when Jess burst in, waggling a urine-soaked stick a little too close to the brewing beverage for my liking, sporting a wide-eyed, almost maniacal grin.

"Benny," she says; (please don't tell anyone she calls me that in private), "I'm pregnant!"

I stopped dunking the teabag and froze, looking back at her with a similar wide-eyed expression. Isaac stood between us, knee-height, wondering what the heck his parents were doing staring at each other with what could only be described as chronic astigmatism.

So there we are, recoiling from the news, and wondering how to react. Some people react by jumping with joy, and some are a little more cautious. It all depends on your nature and the circumstances. Last time, with Isaac, we did the jumping for joy thing: on  my way to work one morning, Jess sent me a photo message of a positive pregnancy test, with the words "Ready to be a dad?!" underneath. Like a fool, I read the message whilst driving, which is almost definitely against the law. I nearly drove off the road.

There's a reason we reacted cautiously this time around, and I'll get this part over and done with. Jess got pregnant in December of 2008, but we unfortunately suffered a miscarriage on Boxing Day. In a way, if you have to have a miscarriage, we had it at the best time; the baby was eight weeks old, and so we hadn't felt it kicking or anything - the only indication we had that we were pregnant was a positive test. Jess had started bleeding a couple of days before Christmas, and we'd gone down to A&E on two separate occasions only to be told that they weren't exactly sure what it was and to go home and rest.

Deep down, I think we both knew what had happened, and this was confirmed on Boxing Day by a very solemn Scottish doctor, who gave us the bad news. We were prepared, but nothing can stem the upset that it causes. We decided to keep the 'products', as our baby was affectionately called, and buried them under a rose in the local park amongst a few trees. Losing a baby at any time during pregnancy is a terrible loss, but I suppose we took some comfort in the knowledge that there were other couples who had been through much worse than us, losing their child later in pregnancy or having a stillbirth. I won't drag this out any longer; all I will say is that if your mrs does experience bleeding at any point during the pregnancy, it's always best to go and get it checked out.

So there we were, staring at each other like a couple of gormless idiots, in a hazy concoction of disbelief, excitement, and trepidation. As I said before, we had been trying for a long time, and so this news was pretty unexpected. Obviously, you're in the same boat, and have found out that your partner/wife/one night stand is pregnant – which is, I assume, why you're reading this book. Either that, or you're just really into babies, which is fine to a certain extent.

At the moment, your baby is just a bunch of cells called an embryo, and is burrowing it's way into the uterus of your mrs. It's around this time that pregnancy tests pick up the hormone called human Chorionic Gonadotropin (snigger…gonad), which is fairly easy for the embryo to produce but near enough impossible to say, especially after a few pints of snakebite and with a mouthful of peas. You may or may not have had an inkling before now that there is a baby forming deep within the bowels of your lady friend – the symptoms, if you missed them, include grumpiness, nausea, fatigue, frequent urination, breast tingling, or delayed periods. If you've noticed the last one in this list, then it's a bit weird that you keep a log of your partner's menstrual cycle, and you should probably get out more.

"Thanks for the pie, darling. Also, couldn't help but notice you're two weeks late."

WEEK FIVE

Tact is the best tactic

Chances are, after the initial excitement, you're both going to begin to worry – probably about different things. You may start to get concerned about finances, whereas she is probably going to be freaking out about how big she's going to get, or the labour she'll have to go through in eight months' time; which is probably why it's a good idea not to tell her that the average woman gains around two stone in weight during her pregnancy, or that due to the weight of your child her feet may spread and grow 1-2 sizes. It's best if you never tell her that at all, ever. She'll probably just grow to resent you for impregnating her in the first place.

Seriously, though, it is best just to enjoy the moment and try not to worry. You'll have tonnes of support along the way; not just from family and friends, but from midwives, doctors, nurses…even the government, when she's far gone enough. Right now, the next eight weeks are critical. It's known colloquially as the "danger zone", the twelve-week period when if something is going to go wrong, there's a higher chance that it will. The baby is developing fast, and so make sure your mrs gets the recommended dosage of Folic Acid down her each day to help keep things ticking along smoothly – and keep her away from alcohol, caffeine, smoking, drugs, prostitution, murder, that kind of thing. They're considered to be really quite bad. Whilst your partner may give up things like murder and alcohol, I can't guarantee that you won't be the subject of some form of violent domestic abuse over the next few months as she turns into some kind of Hulk-like, weepy, hormonal monster. Man, this is going to be fun...

"In sickness, and in health..."

WEEK SIX

Oh my...what is that?!

I have some advice for you, fathers: whatever you do, don't look at any photographs of foetuses at this stage of pregnancy. Although the fact that they are about the size and shape of a baked bean sounds cute, they sure as heck don't look it. It sounds mean, and you mustn't mention this to your partner, but right now your baby looks like something straight out of an *Alien* movie. It might not be *Alien*, it could of course be *Aliens*, or *Alien 3*; maybe *Alien Resurrection*, or *Alien vs Predator*...but you get the gist. All I'm saying is, if you can see a resemblance of yourself in your baby at this stage, you quite urgently need to visit a plastic surgeon.

Breastfeeding would be a bad choice.

My second piece of advice, and a quiet word in your ear, if you will: the mother of your child is already well aware that chances are she will put on a bit of weight whilst she's pregnant. I'm not talking just the weight of the baby itself, I mean actual fat. I know you already know what I am about to tell you, but always always *always* tell her that she does not look fat, no matter how...*voluptuous* she may become. One day, perhaps soon, her bum actually *will* look big in that; but you must never say.

We went for an early scan today, something which is pretty normal if you've suffered a miscarriage before. Fortunately, there's a heartbeat; we got a 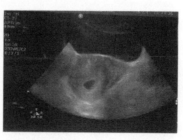 little print-out of the scan, although it barely shows anything. At present, my child is but a small white fleck in a writhing mass of grey.

They also told us that instead of six and a half weeks pregnant, we're five and a half weeks pregnant, which thoroughly confused me to the point where I wanted to curl up and hibernate for the next eight months whilst gibbering "No more numbers...no more numbers..." under my breath. We're not sure who to believe; Jess knows her periods inside out, which in itself is revolting, and is certain that we are six and a half weeks. The midwives have made this mistake before...when Isaac was born, two days earlier than his due date, his hands and feet were very dry – indicative of an overdue baby – which resulted in us having to rub extra virgin olive oil into his extremities for the first few weeks of his life; in itself resulting in a child who smelt like chips. Who knows when this next little blighter will arrive?

A week later, and we have another scan just to double check everything's OK. Fortunately, it is, and the baby's grown a fair bit now, the heartbeat being a lot clearer. Wiped brows all round!

A tip, kind of related to one I made earlier about your mrs' weight: your partner/the mother of your child will often, when out and about with your good self, point to another lady and ask "Am I skinnier than she is?". Now, I know you know this already, but the answer is always 'Yes', even if the poor person in her sights is the skinniest, most anorexic beanpole you've ever seen. If you say 'No', then rest assured all hell will break loose. You may be tempted to say it, like the way you're tempted to respond sarcastically when the man with the big gun at the airport asks if you're carrying any explosives or knives; but don't. You probably won't end up in jail for ten years if you're sarcastic to your lady friend, but after she's finished with you you'll wish you were.

Right now, that bunch of embryonic cells in your mrs' belly is beginning to form a distinct shape, about 2mm in length, looking kind of like a slightly elongated baked bean, with a bulge in the middle which will eventually form your baby's heart. Its brain and nervous system are developing quickly, and optic vessels – which will form the eyes – are appearing on the side of its head. The digestive and respiratory systems are also beginning to form, as are small buds which will grow into arms and legs. Finally, and perhaps the most incredible, is that the heart kicks into life around week six and begins to beat.

There's a few things your mrs should avoid (apart from the obvious, like skydiving or running across a minefield), especially concerning food: she should steer well clear of things like soft cheeses, unpasteurised milk, raw meat, food containing raw eggs, shellfish or pâté. All of these things run the risk of illnesses such as listeriosis and toxoplasmosis, which can cause birth defects or miscarriage. There's also a risk that toxoplasmosis can be contracted from soiled cat litter, so if you have a cat, it's now your exclusive job to scoop up the poo, you lucky thing.

It's law at this point for your partner's employer to carry out an assessment if her job involves a risk to her pregnancy. If a risk is found, then she can be transferred to another job or task, with no loss of pay.

These first few weeks are a strange time. Neither of you may believe that you are pregnant, and perhaps not be as excited as you think you should be. Your mrs may be grumpy (or grumpier than usual) on account of the hormones swilling around her system. She is probably also constantly complaining about sore boobs, in which case you should go out and buy her a comfy pregnancy bra. Seriously, it'd gain you untold brownie points and – for a moment, at least – you can bask in the light of being some kind of bra-buying hero. She also might mention that her areolas are darker, in which case just turn up your nose slightly and edge away.

You can also be some kind of cape-clad superman by simply helping out around the house, as your mrs is probably feeling knackered already (although watch out for signs of deliberate exaggeration in order to obtain extravagant sympathy and/or numerous cups of caffeine-free tea). Her senses are also heightened during pregnancy, especially her sense of smell. You know they say a shark can smell a teaspoon of blood in a swimming pool? Well your mrs can smell a fart in a warehouse, no joke. Therefore, it's best to keep strong smells of all kinds away from her to minimise the risk of her chucking up all over your nice carpet.

Here's a revolting fact: some people drink the urine of pregnant women as they believe it boosts their immune system. Please, please don't. It's really gross and there's always other ways of fortifying your body, ways that taste much nicer and don't run the risk of you being completely rejected by society and disowned by your family.

WEEK SEVEN

It's a plug, but there's no chain

During this week your baby has a bit of a growth spurt, jumping from 3mm at the start of the week (about the size of a grain of rice) to 11-13mm by the end. The buds that are arms and legs now have 'plates' at the end of them, with tiny bumps that are beginning to separate into fingers and toes. Numerous other body parts are also forming rapidly this week, including eyelids, eye lenses, bladder, tongue, liver, lungs – you name it, it's probably growing (within reason, of course).

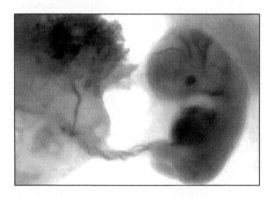

Your baby is actually in the process of using its second set of kidneys, with three separate sets being grown over the months of your baby's development. Your partner's kidneys are also working overtime to process all the extra waste, which – when coupled with the cauldron of hormones swimming through her veins – makes her wee endlessly. Your child is also moving around, but your partner won't be able to feel it yet.

Your mrs has also developed a mucous plug, which forms at the opening of her cervical canal and protects against infection. It's also as gross as it sounds, and it comes free during labour - so if you're a really lucky boy you might get to see it, in which case chances are you'll be spending your time dry retching into the sink as your partner squeezes a child through her bits.

Nothing like a bath plug, unfortunately. And there's no chain.

WEEK EIGHT

Fingers crossed...

"Our baby looks gross." states my wife, as she squints at a photo on the internet, nostrils flared slightly in a sickly grimace. "Kind of like a deformed alien."

I look at the photo, and am inclined to agree. Although it is looking more and more like a person each day, you'd still look twice if it walked past you in the street. Still, we love it already, and why not? Looks aren't everything, which is why ugly people sometimes find love, although it is understandably rare.

Jess' pregnancy has been quite 'easy' so far – I've put easy in inverted commas, as if you're ever to tell a bloated woman her pregnancy is 'easy' you're in for a good hiding. She has felt sick but not actually been sick, but that may be because she has read that eating boiled sweets helps to relieve sickness. Also, they just so happen to be really tasty.

She read this little titbit of advice on a dedicated website to expectant mothers. I won't name names for fear of endorsing a product (I love Pepsi) but there are some great websites around with endless forums where  engorged ladies can discuss every pregnancy and parenting topic under the sun. It's great for them to get into girly chatter, so that they can 'share their feelings', or whatever they do, plus it gets them out of your hair for a while so you can watch the footy.

At this point during pregnancy, your baby's junk is beginning to form, although it is still too soon to find out if it is a boy or a girl. All together now, dads; fingers crossed (c'mon, boy...boy...). This is all going on inside a uterus which is about the size of an orange. If your partner is beginning to freak about how big a bump she's going to have, I suggest you sit back supinely and calmly float across the fact that by the end of her pregnancy your mrs' uterus will have swelled to 500 times its normal size. Then throw your head back and laugh, like a madman or a baddie in superhero films. Now would also be a good time to tell her that due to those darn hormones she may well break out in a few spots (which will go after the first trimester, but don't mention that just yet). Then laugh again, but keep your distance.

"We shall call him...Number Two."

You can make amends by accompanying your partner to any prenatal appointments she may have around this time, and getting involved. Ask a million questions, to the point where you can tell that the midwife/doctor wants to hit you but is commanded by the laws of the land to not do so. Then, by the end of it, you'll be an expert on pregnancy and you can take your mrs out for a caffeine and alcohol-free drink to celebrate – that is, if she's not too tired. Her body is undergoing some big changes and as a result she may become fatigued quickly, in which case the best thing you can do is look after the house/kids/dog and give her a good nap. She'll thank you through the medium of snores.

WEEK NINE

Rainbow yawns, and a hole in my wallet

The morning sickness has now struck Jess with aplomb, causing her to blow chunks on a regular basis right in the middle of a weekend visiting old family friends (I hope she managed to get it all inside the toilet). She's also experiencing quite sharp abdomen pains, which we know from when she was pregnant with Isaac is as a result of her having a double hernia operation when she was a baby; the scar tissue is giving her grief as her ligaments stretch to accommodate her swelling womb. At the moment, your baby is about three centimetres long, inside a sac which is about the size of a hen's egg.

Exhibit A: a hen's egg.

Disclaimer: If your mrs has pains, it is best to see your doctor. Now don't sue me.

Anyway, this pain is causing her to whinge a bit, prompting me, in the end, to grumpily mutter "Get over it". I'm not being mean, it's just that during the same evening I'd had an unfortunate encounter with a newly-toasted Pop Tart which had resulted in a burnt thumb, which I was nursing carefully and sucking from time to time. Although it's considered safe for her to have paracetamol (but not aspirin or ibuprofen) she's refusing any pain relief just to be on the safe side.

She's also incredibly weepy. A single episode of 'Scrubs', which normally has us both in stitches, today reduced her to a blubbering wreck on account of one song that was played which reminded her of being pregnant with Isaac ('Overkill' by Colin Hay, if you must know). I am being as supportive as possible, but as I suffer from a ridiculously short attention span it gets tricky. Exasperated, Jess tells me that if I was pregnant for a day I'd be the most "whinging man ever". I tell her maybe so, but at least I wouldn't do it out loud.

Us men are not without our pain, though: recently Jess spent £250 on maternity clothes. They're necessary as she's already got a bit of a bump and  therefore needs to cover herself up until we tell people, and so she'll get good use out of them – but it still doesn't stop the whole thing being flipping expensive.

Jess has low blood pressure, and so suffers now and again from dizzy spells during pregnancy. This is quite normal around this time, so keep alert and make sure that she gets plenty of food and water to keep her going. You may also need to either pluck her out of the air if she faints or turn her over into the recovery position if she passes out completely, which for my weedy arms is quite a task.

OK, so she just cried at an episode of 'Friends'. What the hell's going on?!

It wasn't even that episode where Ross and Rachel split up.
Stop it, I'm getting teary.

WEEK TEN

Breaking the news, and the cheesecake conundrum

They've all gone to pot, our timescales. I don't know if I'm coming or going. I spend my minutes in a wide-eyed stupor as I look fleetingly around the room, knees huddled by my chin.

OK, so maybe I'm being a bit melodramatic; but we've had to tell people two weeks early. I'm not actually that bothered about it, I just thought I'd turn my hand to some gripping writing. Turns out I'm ace at it.

But yes, the cat's out of the bag.

This cat, however, remains in the bag.

My mother-in-law guessed that Jess was pregnant using her mother's intuition and her eyes (Jess' bump is getting big already. I hope it's mostly fluid, otherwise I'm expecting a gargantuan beast of a baby in a few months' time. Boy, I would not like to push *that* out). Jess was caught off guard, and the truth was revealed. For the sake of fairness, we told my family as well. This is pretty much how it panned out.

We went to my mum's house first. We brainstormed vehemently during the twenty minute journey, concluding that the best way of delivering the news was to give her a birthday card signed "from Ben, Jess, Isaac and your second grandchild" - it was her birthday a couple of days earlier, you see. We weren't just buying her a birthday card out of the blue; that would have frazzled her already ageing brain and probably plunged her into Alzheimer's. She read the card and initially had quite a mellow reaction.

"Oh, it's another crossword scenario, is it?" she said, with a grin on her face. Don't get too embroiled in the crossword thing; it's how we told her about Jess' pregnancy with Isaac, and is a long story. I'll tell you, one day.

It was only when my youngest sister read the card and started whooping like some kind of startled jungle monkey that my mother joined in, obviously spurred on by her now-gasping daughter. Seeking refuge from the living room – which by this point sounded like the depths of the Amazon – I went upstairs to ring my dad.

Just as I told him the news, the line went deathly silent. I had images of my father clutching his mobile, his jaw on his lap, breath wheezing in grandfatherly pride. Instead, it turned out to be a dropped signal, as he came back on the line mid-sentence. Oh well – my dad never was one for thespian reactions, but he was still thrilled.

How I imagine his face looked, just with less hair.

Next, I rang my other sister, who was settling in at uni.

"Hi, are you sober?" I open with, chuckling at my own inimitable wit – although I was being a bit serious, despite it being only six in the evening. Freshers week, you see. Anyway, I tell her the good news, and she screams for nigh on three whole minutes.

Next, we drive to Jess' sister, who is recovering from knee surgery and was just about conscious enough to congratulate us. Finally, the grandparents, who are excited but in a calm way, so as to stave off heart attacks, strokes, high blood pressure, that kind of thing.

The next day, I'm at my office desk wondering about how to tell girly news in a manly way. In the end, I make my decision, plan my strategy, fill out the relevant forms and execute my action points. I lean back in my chair and face my colleague and good friend Gordon: an ageing, balding, rather lanky man who wears glasses and sounds like he's sucking on peanut butter when he eats.

"My mrs is pregnant, Gordon, and I think it's yours." I state, deadpan. "Reason being, we only have sex once a year, and that was back in February."

The word is out and overheard, and the gruff congratulations from my male colleagues are peppered with the excited squeals of their female counterparts, whose heads pop up above partitioning as their keen bat-ears eavesdrop on my announcement. I accept their best wishes with a big grin, and secretly hope that they buy me cakes and a pint to celebrate.

At around ten weeks you'll be invited to a 'booking in' appointment with your midwife, which for us was down at the local hospital. During this meeting they'll give you your green notes, which is a booklet which contains everything relating to the pregnancy and is, perhaps unsurprisingly, a green colour.

Just a warning: during this appointment they ask endless questions, about pretty much everything to do with your life. Questions such as "Do you have or have you ever had herpes?" and "Is the child Ben's?" – which made me listen intently. Fortunately, it is.

I had a witty answer in my mind to every question asked, especially the ones about mental health and the minefield of a question "Are you related?". "Yes, she's my mother!" I longed to scream with childish glee, but fortunately for everyone I abstained.

There was one point during the incessant questioning where I could hold back no longer. The midwife was listing foods that Jess should keep away from: swordfish, shark, peanuts, pâté...and then she mentioned soft cheese. She reeled off Brie, Camembert, ticking each one off on a podgy finger. She was just about to carry on, when I took my chance.

"You're partial to cheese-CAKE, aren't you?" I say, turning to look intently at Jess; who looks back, po-faced.

"I-erm-not really..." she whispers, leaning in to my Cheshire-cat face. I know full well that she's not a big cheesecake fan, but continue nonetheless.

"Is that safe...cheesecake?" I say, looking at the midwife, who has a bewildered expression.

"Umm...yes..." she says, slowly, probably assessing my mental history in her own mind as she eyes me up and down. I sit back in my chair, arms folded, smug expression.

The midwife, after weighing Jess and measuring her height, packs her off to pee into a tiny tube; leaving just us in the room. I think of possible conversation topics, but she is scribbling intently on Jess' forms, obviously faking to avoid talking to me, so I let her scribble. After a few minutes Jess returns, proudly clutching a small vial of golden liquid, and plonks it triumphantly on the midwife's desk. Her complacent expression is soon drained when the midwife explains that she is now going to take a blood sample - Jess has quite the phobia of needles, often passing out whenever approached for an injection. When we were pregnant with Isaac and she had blood taken, it took fifteen minutes of sitting down in the hospital corridor and three Crème Eggs before she was able to walk to the car.

 This time, however, she was very brave. She told me afterwards that she managed to stave off unconsciousness by thinking about the route she was going to run the next day. She was an avid runner before we got pregnant but stopped when we found out, as we weren't sure how much exercise she could have. It turns out that exercise in moderation is fine, half an hour tops though. After taking what seems to be about twelve tubes of blood, the appointment is over and I usher the slightly woozy wife to the door.

"Come on you." I say, soothingly. "Let's go get you some cheesecake."

Your baby has now begun to 'breathe' the amniotic fluid, and it also urinates – which is absorbed into your partner's system and comes out when she pees. Her blood volume is also increasing by 40-50%, which is why you might be able to notice veins beneath the skin that you hadn't seen before. These will return to normal following birth, but be sensitive to the fact that your mrs might be panicking that her chest looks like a road map and shower her with compliments.

Oh, congratulations by the way: your baby (measuring about an inch now from crown to rump) is no longer an embryo but has levelled up to foetus status – and no longer has a tail. Result!

WEEK ELEVEN
Butterflies

Jess is not feeling too great at the moment. The vomiting seems to have stopped, but she's feeling generally rough; she looks it too, although I wouldn't tell her without leaving at least two arm lengths between us. I'm lavishing sympathy and support on her in abundance, buying her pregnancy magazines and the like as she flakes on the sofa. Who would have thought being pregnant would make me so knackered as well!

By the way, it is not advisable when your partner is in a state of discomfort to indicate using your hands how big the child is going to be in just a few months' time. Despite being laid flat out, Jess can still cause my testicles to wither and contract with just one glare.

You're probably going to laugh at me when I say this, but we felt the baby moving this week. I can hear you scoffing from here: "Eleven weeks?" you cry incredulously. "But the average pregnant beauty doesn't feel the baby kicking until at least week 17!"

But wipe that little bubble of dribble off the page, dear reader, and read on. Bear in mind this is Jess' second pregnancy. It is common for ladies in their second pregnancy to show (or "pooch", which is an awesome word) earlier than in their first pregnancy – and they can also feel the baby moving earlier. If you don't believe me, take a quick glance at the internet through Google or another reputable search engine and then slump in your chair when you realise I'm right. Anyway, it was a very surreal experience and really brought home what's going on. Not panicking just yet, but I do have a bad case of the pit sweats.

As demonstrated by this guy.

If things are beginning to break you out into a sweat, make sure you take a little time for yourself whilst still letting your mrs know you're there for her and supporting her. Play a round of golf, go to a football match, head down the pub...it'll certainly help if your head's a bit of a mess. Go easy on the pints though; the last thing your partner needs is you sharing the toilet bowl with her whilst you're both barfing away.

Do me a favour, and stick out your little finger. That's about the length of your baby right now, a baby who also proudly boasts a fully formed pair of ears. The head is disproportionately large in relation to the body, and accounts for about half the total length. (This is normal, by the way, and doesn't necessarily mean you have some kind of Einstein on your hands.)

The umbilical cord is also fully formed, and is working hard to give nourishment to your child as well as taking all waste products away. The mini-you has also learned to swallow, and bizarrely may have some intestines projecting from its abdomen and into the umbilical cord. Quit shrieking, it's perfectly normal, and they will return to the abdomen within the next fortnight. I'm sorry, I shouldn't have freaked you like that – I'll be more careful in future.

Although it was pretty funny.
(PS. This is another type of 'pooch')

Things are moving fast at the moment, and by the end of the week Freddie Foetus will have doubled in size to two inches. That's two times one inch, for those who have trouble with doubles. That rhymed. Unintentional.

WEEK TWELVE

Yeah, that's probably just sweat

Many of the pregnancy books that I have read and the articles I've skimmed through on the internet talk of a "pregnancy glow" around this time. As I look up from my laptop and eye my wife tentatively, I see nothing of this fabled glow. Instead, my wide-eyed gaze lingers upon the hormonal snarl that is the mother of my child as she wipes away another chocolate goatee, caused by a poor bar of Galaxy that didn't know what hit it.

I'm being unfair: you see, we are moving house next week, and so a lot of our time has been spent endlessly packing our life belongings into flimsy boxes; and this has left Jess exhausted. On top of this, she is recovering from a urine infection, which is very common during pregnancy, on account of hormone changes affecting the urinary tract and slowing down the flow of urine – ironic, seeing as she is peeing like a horse about a million times a day. It seems to have resolved itself without antibiotics, which would normally be prescribed before the infection spread to the kidneys and caused possible pregnancy complications such as a smaller than usual child or early labour (a risk that arises later on in pregnancy).

Having skimmed through what I've written so far, it sounds like I'm being very mean about my wife. I would take a quick estimate that about 100% of what I've penned relating to her makes her out to be some kind of large-breasted, hormonal banshee. She's not (apart from the large breasts). She's an incredibly good mother to Isaac, and a cracking wife. She works very hard for the family and throws herself into everything she does, which often means she finds it difficult just to take a few moments to slob out in front of the TV. The thing is, we (as men) may find it easy to snigger when our partner cries at an episode of *The Tweenies*, but I think I can safely say that if I had an actual living person growing inside my abdomen I would be constantly freaking out, fearing an *Alien*-like scenario where one day I'll wake up and this baby will burst out of my chest and scurry around the room, making high-pitched whiny noises.

OH HAI LOVE ME PLEASE

You're in your twelfth week, which means you're out of the 'danger zone', and now the risk of miscarriage drops dramatically. If all has gone well, your baby's limbs and organs have all formed and now it's just a case of growth and development for the remaining months before it dives out of your partner's birth canal in a haze of mucous and fury. You're also at the end of your first three months, also known as a trimester, which makes it sound like you should be sitting an exam right about now.

"How do you spell 'blastocyst'?!"

Your baby is now about eight centimetres in length, and is growing fast. The placenta which feeds it is totally formed, but will only be working fully in another month or so. If your mrs has experienced morning sickness, this should now begin to fade away, which leaves you with a bit more free time - previously taken up with holding back hair from the toilet pan as your better half throws 3D yawns at the porcelain. The eyelids are now formed but will not open until about seven months in order to protect the sensitive optic nerves. Reflexes are now developed, your baby moves more frequently, and may even suck its thumb. The digestive system is now capable of making contractions that pushes food through the bowels, and is also capable of absorbing sugar. Pretty amazing stuff!

Now is about the time that you would tell friends and family. Whilst this will be a happy time, you should warn your partner that for the next few months her ever-expanding belly will become a hand magnet. She will have people touching her stomach who up until then had barely said hello, and she will rapidly get cheesed off with it. This, 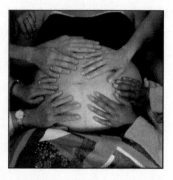 coupled with the ongoing hormone thing, may result in many of your loved ones nursing broken knuckles and a face that looks like someone has played noughts and crosses on it with a rusty nail.

The good news is this: the second trimester is meant to be the best out of the three. This is because the uterus has shifted forward slightly and will not be pressing on your mrs' bladder, so the toilet trips should become less frequent (I would avoid telling her that this comes back with a vengeance during the third trimester). She may actually have the glow which is sadly lacking during our pregnancy, due to the fact that her sebaceous glands are secreting more oil, giving her skin a nice sheen. However, headaches may be more common due to the increased blood volume – as well as light headedness - so if there are any concerns just give your midwife a call and talk things through.

A good activity to do together whilst your partner is feeling a bit better is exercise, such as walking or light jogging. You should stipulate from the start that this does not involve sprinting around department stores shopping for clothes, but instead nice walks where you can enjoy one another's company before things get really noisy and lie-ins become a thing of the past.

You'll also have a dating scan during this week, where for most people they will see their child for the first time. Don't worry if you're both nervous in the build-up to the scan; it's perfectly normal. In times like this your mind goes a bit crazy and you start to convince yourself that your baby has five heads and three feet, that they won't find anything at all, or that they'll come across something random, like a lightbulb.

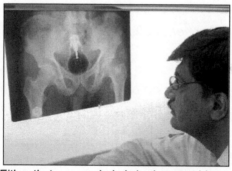

"Either that, or your baby's had a great idea…"

And so, sat there in the hospital waiting room, leafing through well-thumbed magazines from months ago, Jess and I were both a bit anxious. We both needed a wee, but for different reasons; I was a bit nervous, and Jess had just downed a pint of water so that the ultrasound would be clearer – the full bladder pushes the uterus closer to the surface of the abdomen. One thing you'll quickly learn is that chances are you'll never get seen on time, and the sonographer will undoubtedly call you in about fifteen minutes late, by which time your partner may be so ready to burst that she's pulling faces like she's just sucked on a lemon.

Much of this day rides on the sonographer you have. If you get a good one, the whole experience will be a lot more rewarding than some of the sour-faced old witches we've had in the past. When we had the miscarriage we had the standard scan just to check how far progressed everything was. Let me recreate the moment for you, just quickly:

> *Jess and I enter the ultrasound room, nervous and upset.*
>
> *Sonographer pushes her little ultrasound wand thing about.*
>
> *"Nope, there's no pregnancy in the womb." She declares, with all the compassion of Hitler.*
>
> *We leave the ultrasound room.*

However, I'm pleased to report that the sonographer we had during this scan was excellent. The worst thing about most sonographers is that for the first few seconds of the ultrasound, when the picture on the monitor is a swirling mass of black and grey, they will say nothing; during which, you're both invariably thinking "Umm, is there a problem?!" and getting yourselves even more stressed.

Our sonographer told us that she was going to take a look around the womb before she took a close look at the baby, which she did. Then, suddenly, Baby Wakeling came into view. Now, before we'd gone into the scan, I was thinking about funny things I could put into this book; but all of that went out of the window when I saw the little guy or girl on the screen. You know now as well as I do that it is one of the most surreal experiences ever. It was asleep when we had our scan, but every now and again it rubbed its face or gave a little kick. You see everything; arms, legs, hands, feet, right down to little fingers, thumbs and toes, and it's one of the most amazing things ever. You basically just sit there, open-mouthed, as your tongue gets drier and drier.

The sonographer will take a few measurements and give you a firm due date, and an exact date of how far gone you are – in our case, 12 weeks and 4 days. The scan also confirmed that a cyst that showed up on our earlier scan had disappeared. If a cyst shows up on your mrs' scan, don't be too alarmed; they're very common during pregnancy and often just shrivel up and die.

Next comes the showing of the scan photo to friends and family. By the way, I should warn you – they often charge for the photos. We had to pay a tenner for three, which was a lot better than last time, when we had to pay £15 for two. Darn NHS. At least it's fun to watch people you know squint and wrinkle their noses as you proudly shove the scan photo in their faces. You'll undoubtedly have to point out various limbs, but for the most part the photos are fairly clear.

 Jess' appetite has diminished lately, which may well stave off the inevitable 'Jabba the Hut' look that was a very dangerous possibility during the first few weeks. I've done a bit of research, and it turns out you don't actually have to 'eat for two' during the first six months of pregnancy at all, despite what your old Aunt Bessie tells you as she pushes more pork chops in your direction. In fact, even after six months your lady friend only needs to increase her intake by 200 calories a day, which is equivalent to one piece of toast and a banana. The moral of the story is this: if your mrs is hoarding chocolate, guzzling on cake and using pregnancy as an excuse, snatch the bar of Cadburys from her hand, slap her wrist and take it for yourself. You're a growing boy, after all.

The whole moving house thing is stalling as per usual, which isn't surprising. This added stress, combined with Jess' heightened emotions, has resulted in many a solicitor having their ear chewed by a shrieking and sobbing pregnant harpy spitting venom down the phone. A lot of the time this has led to tears, not just from Jess but undoubtedly from the solicitor as well, who – as I imagine it –

hangs up the phone and sobs manically for ten minutes straight, forehead on desk whilst bewildered colleagues try unsuccessfully to comfort their co-worker. Or fire comes out of the phone receiver and burns up their face: one of the two.

Stress can, however, affect your baby, so try and make sure if there is something going on that's heaping stress on you and your mrs that you take most of the burden. Tests have proved that foetuses are receptive to the mother's stress hormones and this can adversely impact their brain and development. This may explain why I have no common sense, or why I'm so pants at football. Either that, or I'm inbred.

WEEK THIRTEEN

What do you mean, you don't know why?

What a week. We've had nose bleeds, torn muscles, exhaustion, and diarrhoea. Actually, that's all me, apart from the diarrhoea bit, although with the swine flu that's going around it could be a very real possibility. We moved house this week, which meant flexing my puny muscles and putting them through more grief than they've ever known before. At the end of moving day, I could practically hear my weedy biceps screaming "WHAT THE HELL JUST HAPPENED?!"

Anyway, this isn't about me; it's about the mrs. She has had the odd nose bleed, on account of the increased blood volume. And she is exhausted, on account of the person growing inside her. She also has the odd bout of sciatica, which is very common around this time during pregnancy.

She's also crying, a *lot*. Whereas before she cried at sitcoms, she now cries at nothing. Absolutely nothing. I have just returned from consoling her as she blubbered in the bath for no reason at all. Never mind – 'theirs is not to reason why, theirs is but to do and die', as someone once said at some point in the history of time, maybe after having just cried in the bath.

She's also freaking a bit that the general public doesn't realise she's pregnant and just thinks she's fat. This is especially concerning for her when she goes out running, because she reckons people will see her and think "Aah, look at that fat person waddling down the street. At least she's trying to lose weight. Most fatties just eat burgers and wallow in their own filth."

"Must...get – to KFC – before closing...time."

This has prompted her to wear one of her newly-acquired shirts whilst out jogging; you know the ones, with a whimsical saying on the front, like 'Does my bump look big in this?' or something similar. She might as well be wearing a massive flashing neon sign on her back saying "HEY! STOP STARING! I'M PREGNANT, NOT FAT!".

Wow, that's a lot of capital letters I've written in the last few paragraphs. I must have a lot of pent-up anger or something, which will almost certainly not be channelled into sustained DIY. Changing a light bulb is about as far as I go, and even then it's often a case of accidentally buying a bayonet cap when in reality it's screw.

Your baby is about the length of a credit card, moving more now, and a quick bit of research has revealed that it is also smiling and grimacing, although what exactly it has to grimace at I'm not sure. Mind you, if I was swimming in a sac of goo, with a big tube sticking out of my abs, I'd be pulling a bit of a face too. Toenails have formed, and it's body is covered in a soft downy hair called lanugo, which remains until the last few weeks of pregnancy, when the baby eats it (gross). Apparently, your baby uses the umbilical cord as it's first toy around now, but I'm not sure how. Maybe like a whip, à la Zorro. Who knows?

Hands off, foetus. I've already called shotgun on Catherine Zeta-Jones.

WEEK FOURTEEN

You married it, you lucky thing

I've just stepped out of the shower, and watched as my wife is visibly repulsed by me. Disheartening for any man, but fortunately she isn't revolted by my body - and, of course, there's no reason why she should be – instead her continued super-sense of smell has picked up the tiniest whiff of shower gel I've used and her big bloodhound snout is overwhelmed. I have the last laugh, though. When I'm asleep I dream wonderful dreams, like being a groupie for *Girls Aloud*, or picking off Nazis in 1941, Jess is having frequent nightmares, mostly about the baby, but now and again the odd one about me. If the same is happening to your mrs, continued hugs should do the trick, despite it being 3 in the morning.

My wife is so grumpy, not least because we're having issues in the new house and can't get a decent TV reception or the internet. After a while, every *Scrubs* episode on DVD kind of merges into one. Plus, we're watching endless repeats of *Spot the Dog*, which is Isaac's current favourite. That damn music sticks in your head and will not let go. You'll see.

WEEK FIFTEEN

Funny how she's only craving nice things

Apparently, Jess has insomnia, or so she tells me; I wouldn't know, I sleep through it. This is a very common condition during pregnancy, which can be caused by actual medical conditions causing discomfort, such as sinus congestion, backache or carpal tunnel syndrome, or something as simple as having an overactive mind with everything that's going on. If it is caused by a condition, the best thing to do is point your mrs in the general direction of your midwife or GP. Otherwise, gentle exercise can help, as well as other remedies such as aromatherapy – although make sure that no more than three drops at a time are used and that essential oils are used with caution in the first trimester. They can be added to a warm bath, or a few drops on her pillow before bedtime. Other tips suggest imagining you're in a beautiful countryside,  or – as one website mooted – counting backwards in sevens from 1,000, which I think would probably not send me to sleep but instead make my brain melt and my eyes pop out.

She also has a craving for wine gums, of all things. She's ploughed her way through two boxes already today and is showing no signs of slowing up. It's not even like she wants them; she *has* to have them, like wine gums are her heroin and I'll catch her one day injecting one of the green ones into her forearm, or heating the black one on a spoon with foil and smoking it, or whatever it is you do with drugs. She's really obsessive about it, smacking my hand away when I try to take one and even lashing out with a foot at one point, which only narrowly averted my gonads thanks to some quick thinking and deft hipwork. I can only liken it to a lioness defending a kill, just more ferocious and slightly less hairy.

"The black ones are the best, nom nom nom"

Decoration going slowly; it seems thinking about it doesn't quite work, although my wife has a glare that could strip wallpaper.

Some women around this time will begin to show some pigmentation, such as darker nipples and – oddly – a dark line down the centre of their abdomen. This is more noticeable in olive or dark-skinned women; I'm yet to think of the benefits of a strange stomach line, or ways in which I could use it in some kind of belly drawing. A lot of women around this time find themselves to be constipated, although if you know that kind of thing you two should probably consider not sharing quite so much information.

Your baby's crown-to-rump length is about four inches, and it is growing at an amazing rate. It has translucent skin, which means that the blood vessels are visible; also, the eyebrows and head hair are continuing to grow, with the cells which produce dark hair colour kicking in about now. Apparently, the amniotic fluid – which is a constant half degree Celsius above your partner's body temperature – can smell strongly of curry, cumin, garlic, onion and other essences, depending on what she's eaten. Tell her to back off the spag bol; how would you like to soak in a bath of garlic water?!

"Whaaat?! It'll make me invincible against vampires; but, unfortunately, irresistible to the French."

WEEK SIXTEEN

Time to clingfilm the carpet

How the hell is it only sixteen weeks? It feels like Jess has been pregnant for decades. Her bump is now a proper pregnancy bump, but that doesn't stop her worrying about muffin tops, bat wings or turkey neck because well, let's face it, she's a woman; and the only women who don't fret on a daily basis about their appearance are either stunningly gorgeous supermodels, two year-olds or those who are so incredibly ugly there's no point even trying.

Even Barbie freaks out sometimes about wrinkles and saggy buttocks.

Around this time you should have another midwife appointment, for which your mrs will need to once again pee into a small tube without either the aid of a funnel or the convenience of a penis. During this appointment they will check the heartbeat and measure the baby. Our midwife did neither of these things for some reason, instead confining us to her stuffy overheated office whilst she mumbled through her notes and answered questions with hazy and wayward answers. "Drink milk." she replies, when Jess asks her what she can do to help cure her insomnia. (Surely that's a better answer for the question "How do I get a funny white moustache?") When you go for your appointment, make sure that a) the midwife is half decent, and b) that they actually do what they're meant to. We will now have to wait for another fortnight until our 3D scan to know for sure that everything's OK, which is very exciting because we find out whether our baby will have a dinkle or a tuppence.

Or neither, like Ken.

At some point you and your partner will need to talk about and agree on a birth plan – and by agree on, I mean that you object pathetically before eventually giving in with much less fight than you should have. With Isaac, our firstborn, we opted for a hospital birth, as many mothers do, and rightly so; if you're having a new experience such as childbirth, you want to be in the safest place possible. With this baby, Jess is really excited about the prospect of a home birth; me, not so much. I'm a worrier, taking after my mother, who can expertly turn the tiniest thing into the largest catastrophe with just a simple raised pitch to her voice and the occasional forehead-in-hand moment. However, I think I have reacted in the same way as most people: a home birth is all well and good, but if something goes wrong, you want to be in a hospital. Plus, when your mrs spurts goo, blood and the occasional turd within a three-foot radius I would much rather it be some underpaid person with a mop cleaning it up off a smooth hospital floor instead of me with a can of Vanish trying to grind it out of a deep pile carpet.

A bit of research was needed, and it yielded some interesting results: only about 2% of women have a home birth, mostly due to the fact that it was discouraged in the 1950s due to poor general health in the country and unhygienic housing conditions. However, there are many benefits of a home birth, including a less painful labour, one-to-one care, more privacy and lower rates of postnatal infections for mother and baby. The mother is often more relaxed during the labour due to familiar surroundings, and this relaxation produces endorphins which reduce pain, instead of adrenaline which interrupts labour hormones and makes labour slower and more painful. Plus, if anything were to go wrong – and, with Jess being low-risk, it shouldn't – an ambulance will be at the house in four minutes or less. If any doctor, nurse or midwife thinks at any point during your pregnancy that you are at higher risk of complications, they will encourage a hospital birth. Similarly, if you opt for a home birth and there are difficulties, they will get her to a hospital straight away instead of attempting to coax the child out of your mrs using a pair of BBQ tongs, your finest cutlery, or a vacuum cleaner.

If dual cyclone technology doesn't get it out, nothing will.

If it means that Jess is more relaxed and therefore the labour is a bit easier, then it's fine with me, as long as I'm happy in my own mind. I just hope I have enough time to put a tarpaulin down first.

***

"I can't really be bothered with labour." I sigh, as Jess turns and looks at me, gobsmacked. "It's just such a faff."

Jess makes some rather strange gulping sounds on account of her incredulity, rather like the sounds I imagine a fish out of water would make if you listened really closely. I sit, arms folded, chin on chest, exhaling slowly.

"Well, I'm sorry it's such an inconvenience for you." she retorts, her voice dripping so much with sarcasm that my ears are getting wet. She can't help but let out a laugh, and I do the same. We're going a bit stir crazy, you see, as we've been sat in the hospital A&E waiting room for the best part of an hour. Jess hasn't felt the baby move for a day or so, and all the pregnancy books are telling us to get it checked out. And so we are. And it seems that the day we have chosen to get the baby checked out is the one day that pretty much everyone has decided to have either an accident or an emergency.

There's a young girl - early teens - in full horse riding gear, her left arm in an improvised sling. There's another girl, this one probably mid-twenties, with a cut above her left eye suffered during – I deduce by her attire – a hockey match. There's people that don't even look ill, but are somehow seen by the doctor before us even though they came in after. And there's the shaven-headed guy in a wheelchair next to me, huffing and puffing because he wasn't admitted to the ward to be observed overnight, even though to the naked eye there's absolutely no reason why he would be, except to perhaps cure a terminal case of the grumps.

Finally, we are called through, and a foreign doctor with a voice frequency lower than that of normal human perception and an accent so thick you could spread it on toast gets a foetal monitor kit and applies some gel to Jess' belly as she lies on a bed which still harbours a blood stain from the previous patient. Mmm, sanitary. All three of us listen in carefully at the strange sounds emanating from the machine, like radio static. Finally, after a nail-biting few minutes, the familiar whoosh-whoosh-whoosh of the baby's heartbeat can be heard and there are sighs of relief all round. After paying the ridiculously high parking fee, which undoubtedly hurt much more than falling off a horse or getting a hockey stick in the eye, we drive home.

Your mrs may get the offer of a maternal blood screening test, which measures the level of various hormones to check whether your baby is at risk of having neural tube defects such as spina bifida or chromosomal problems such as Down syndrome. The latest stats show that out of every 1,000 women who take these tests, about 50 will have abnormal results, and only one or two women will actually have babies with a problem.

Your partner may be able to feel the baby moving around this time, a fluttering in the stomach (much like the feeling she probably had on your first date, you stud). Don't worry if she doesn't feel anything, as the 'quickening' (as this is called) will come in its own time.

Jess' sciatica is really playing up this week, and she's hobbling around like an arthritic pensioner. Hot baths relieve it for a bit, as do – allegedly – two bowls of Coco Pops, but in the end she has given up and requested physio appointments through our local doctors' surgery. She's a bit grumpy today – or should I say grump*ier* – as she was approached by someone in the park who commented on how ill she looks, even though she feels OK apart from the painful back and leg. Talk about playing with fire: I've no idea how that woman didn't end up entwined in the chains of a swing, or crushed beneath a see-saw. "You're beautiful on the inside." I tell her, soothingly. It doesn't help.

Your baby's up to almost five inches now, and the development of facial muscles means that he or she can now pull expressions such as squinting and frowning; although I don't know what it's got to frown about, unless it can understand bad jokes, in which case it would have good reason to pull a face. Or perhaps it could be the fact that it is peeing every 40-45 minutes; ironic, as whenever I have a bath I pee way more times than that.

That's right...I went there.

WEEK SEVENTEEN
When do we take our clothes off?

Early on in the pregnancy, we bought a yoga DVD specifically designed for mums-to-be. Today, ten weeks later, we finally opened it and tried out this rather bizarre practice.

The thing is, we didn't really take it seriously, and if you do that then you're destined to fail, as well as screwing up your alternate nostril breathing in the process (which is ill-advised when you have a winter cold).

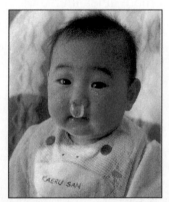

"Relaxation breathing sucks! Now get me a Kleenex."

We began with a section entitled Partner Work, which was basically just like watching really really low-budget pornography, all fully-clothed massages and whatnot. We then moved on to various individual techniques. It's all potentially very helpful stuff, but it's hard to take it seriously when you've got your face in the carpet and your bum in the air whilst trying to perfect calm breathing. It looked like

I'd attempted to body-surf to a shore but instead ended up face first in the sand.

Now I once went to a gym, and so know full well that doing weights hurts a lot, especially when you can't quite manage the barbells and they crush your chest. Trying to get out of that one without drawing unwanted attention was an art form in itself. Anyway, none of that compares to having to crunch your pelvic floor muscles for 30 seconds at a time. Try it: pretend you're holding in pee mid-stream without clenching your buttocks. Hurts, doesn't it? Stupid pelvic floor muscles, stopping me from peeing my pants when I'm old and useless.

"Quit taking a photo and get me a nappy, quick."

WEEK EIGHTEEN

"No, sir, that's the umbilical cord."

This week we went for a private sexing scan, so we could find out what we're having (restricted only to either a boy or a girl, of course, unless something really crazy happened a few months ago). They can be slightly on the pricey side, especially if you opt for a 3D scan – which we didn't – but the service you get is miles better than your usual scans, plus you often get a free DVD and a few photos thrown in.

Whilst in the waiting room I surveyed the vast array of business cards and leaflets and came across one with the following sentence on the front:

"Being pregnant is like taking a wonderful journey arriving at an unknown land full of beautiful surprises!"

Now I don't want to be mean, but whoever wrote that has either never been pregnant or is completely retarded. In my experience, pregnancy is not 'a wonderful journey' but instead nine months of puke, hormones and tears, mixed in with a spattering of sciatica and immense mood swings. The 'unknown land full of beautiful surprises' is actually a delivery room in your local hospital where your child is squeezed out amidst a flood of screams, mucous and pethidine. I'm honestly not trying to put you off, I'm just going by my experiences. Some women take three days to push the sprog out, sometimes a nine-pound baby will practically drop out in five minutes. If your mrs asks, tell her the five-minute scenario is more likely.

Also, her face will probably look like this upon entry into said land.

Finally, we enter the scan room, where a rather friendly sonographer squirts the gel and begins to scan. If you don't want to know what we're having, look away now: although it'll be a pointless exercise because a) you won't know when to look back, and b) I'll be referring to it as 'he' or 'she' for the rest of the book anyway.

Instead of just coming out with it, I'll let you do the legwork and guess for yourself. Let's just say that seeing my unborn child's little scrotum 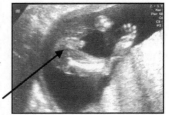 come into view on that fuzzy grey screen was one of the happiest moments of my life. I even got a photo of it to proudly show my parents; plus it'll be fun to watch them turn it upside down, then back the right way again, before figuring out what they're looking at and handing the photo back to me pinched between finger and thumb whilst trying to smile through an upturned nose.

My mrs has rightly said that if we lived in Tudor times she'd be the best wife ever, having already spawned me one heir and harbouring another. There's no way, she says, that she'd be beheaded. I nod along. Not for that at least, I think, but there are a few reasons why she would. Not least just for something to do. I'm pretty sure that's why Henry VIII did it.

"BOOORED! Kill me another wench before I start crying."

Jess had a letter through today offering her a swine flu jab. As yet we're unsure about whether she should have it, and I need to do a bit of geeky research. Hopefully by the time you read this swine flu will have peaked and fizzled out, much like a firework, or the Backstreet Boys. Either that, or it will have wiped out everyone in the world apart from you, in which case I am incredibly pleased that mine is the book you chose to read as everything crumbles around you. Just watch out for the zombies.

In other news, there is a spot underneath the surface on the right side of my nose, quivering like a pubic teenager clutching his first copy of 'Nuts' magazine, just waiting to break through the skin and cause people to keep at least three feet away from me so as to avoid a shot of pus in the eye. Just thought I should warn you.

WEEK NINETEEN

Take your partner by the hand...

This week Jess had her swine flu injection: we came to the conclusion that the risks of having it were a lot lower than the risks of her not having it, namely contracting the aforementioned flu and having a bad case of dying. She is afraid of needles at the best of times, and often feels faint after having either something taken from her body via a syringe or inserted therewith through the same method.

This time, we were not helped by the child screaming in the doctor's surgery room in front of us as we queued nervously outside. This was followed by an old man who walked in, got his shot and walked out within the space of about five seconds, shaking the pain out of his arm as he summoned his obedient wife to follow him out of the surgery. I bet he bypassed the refreshments and mandatory ten minute break that you're meant to have, because he's dead hard and has fought in the Somme.

Beat ya.

Surprisingly, Jess was in and out almost as quickly, although we did take that refreshment break as she started breathing quite heavily - which is almost always a prerequisite to a subsequent collapse and fainting. We were entertained in the waiting room by the brother of the child that had screamed who, at the tender age of about six, said quietly to his sibling, "Can you at least *think* about not crying?"

The next day Jess' arm was dead, and her head was throbbing. It seems that most pregnant women either suffer their first migraine during pregnancy, or, if they have a history of migraines, find they either get worse or better. I'm going to admit, that's probably the most ambiguous and vague piece of information that you'll find in this whole book. To sum up: pregnancy either makes migraines worse, better, or the same. Thanks for reading.

No refunds.

Tonight was the night of a charity do organised by Jess' brothers in order to raise money for sponsorship during next year's London Marathon. Despite a pounding head, the brave mrs still went along, her headache not helped by the music and banter that was quite frankly far too loud. I may be an old man stuck in a 25 year-old's body, but do people have to be quite so raucous when out drinking? What happened to the days of sitting in front of a log fire sipping brandy? People talk and laugh far louder than they would normally when they're out.

Plus, I can't hear myself think – whatever that means.

Anyway, I indulged in a spot of Country Dancing after being egged on by my mother-in-law – and by 'egged on', I mean dragged onto the dance floor. (That woman is ridiculously strong for a fifty-something year-old.) Anyway, I dosey-doed my way through the next ten minutes, spinning women around who I'd never even met before, let alone knowing their names, including some poor young girl who had a cast on her arm. She winced when I high-fived her. Should have probably thought before doing that.

Jess' migraine got worse as the night wore on, and so we went home early. I wasn't too bothered, as

I'd achieved my goal: dancing with a pre-pubescent girl who has a broken arm. Score.

***

Your baby is now covered in a cheesy, white, waxy substance called vernix caseosa, which prevents delicate skin from becoming chapped or scratched, perhaps similar to smothering yourself in cottage cheese. It may sound gross, but if you were mooching around in water for nine months you'd want something to stop you from shrivelling up and looking like a  giant scrotum. As well as this, your child is developing a few layers of fat, to keep it warm. Lately, I have been adding a few layers of my own, and although I have been telling myself that it's for warmth, it's actually because I love bacon sandwiches and I hate any form of exercise.

Baby is now around 15cm long, and – if you're having a girl – her ovaries now contain primitive egg cells. The permanent teeth buds are beginning to form behind the already formed milk teeth buds. Your baby's ears now stand out from the side of its head (hopefully not too much, else it'll look like your mrs is giving birth to the FA Cup), and everything is looking a bit more in proportion now.

Around this time, your mrs may feel the 'quickening' previously mentioned in this book, where she (and you, if your hand is in the right place at the right time) can feel your baby moving. As well as a reassuring and exciting time, this can also be the moment when it suddenly hits you that you're going to be a dad. If you're prone to panicking, please try and rein it in. Going a bit mental and running around crying is probably not going to help matters a lot. Instead, know that your mrs is probably feeling the exact same way, and talk to her about it. You can discuss all aspects of the pregnancy, birth, and beyond – and I can assure you that you'll feel a lot better afterwards. If you're still a little freaked, just rest assured in the fact that at least you don't have to push a seven-pound child out in a few months' time: the worst us men get is a particularly challenging turd after a day of wholemeal bread and bran muffins.

Our panicking face is very similar to our bran muffin-day face.

Your mrs can now ask for a form from her doctor or midwife (currently called a MAT B1 Form), which proves that she's pregnant so that she can claim the relevant benefits and maternity pay. Just in case the massive bump and raging anger hormones aren't proof enough.

WEEK TWENTY

Over the hill

Boom! You're halfway there. The weeks may have gone by in a flash, they may have dragged, but you're on the home straight now. You've done really well so far – breathe slowly, in...out...but don't push. Firstly, you're not the pregnant one. Secondly, it could get messy.

Word of warning: because of the position of the uterus, your mrs' belly button may change shape, or even pop out. During our first pregnancy, Jess' belly button had the misfortune of popping out, and ended up looking like Shrek's ear for the rest of the pregnancy. So far this time, the navel remains an innie, although I'm not going to look too closely in case it shoots out unexpectedly and gets me in the eye.

"I'm gonna dilate THIS much!"

She may also have a little trouble breathing from time to time, but you needn't get big-headed; it's not because of your stunning good looks, or that gut you call a six-pack. It's all down to the pressure on her lungs due to the fact that most of her abdomen is taken up by another person. Pretty freaky when you think about it, isn't it?

Celebrate this halfway milestone by taking her out for a nice meal, or better still buy something for the baby. It'll earn you valuable brownie points and precious ammunition to whip out at an appropriate time at a later date. Not that we do that, of course; as men, all nice things we do are done out of the kindness of our hearts and not with any kind of ulterior motive in mind, not at all.

Thinking 'bout emotional blackmail.

The hair on your baby's scalp is beginning to grow, and it is also practicing breathing movements, although the lungs aren't quite developed enough yet to enable it to breathe outside the womb. You may get another scan around this time, in which case the sonographer is able to tell the sex of the baby, if you so wish.

Jess has SPD, which is certainly not to be confused with an STD, which is something completely different and very suspicious. SPD stands for Symphysis Pubis Dysfunction, and comes about due to your mrs producing the hormone relaxin, which (obviously) relaxes the muscles around the pelvis. As a result, the joints move around more and cause back and hip pain. If it gets too painful, then some physio can ease the discomfort whilst also making her look incredibly daft.

She is also getting a lot of Braxton Hicks contractions, which can come about around this time, or perhaps even earlier. They are tightenings of the uterine muscle, lasting for anywhere from 30 to 60 seconds. A lot of the time, they're painless, but now and again they can cause a bit of discomfort. There are a number of different opinions as to what their purpose is, but many agree that it plays a part in the 'ripening' of your partner's cervix, which is a disgusting mental image. It goes without saying that if these contractions become frequent, very painful and are accompanied by any kind of discharge (eww) then get down to A&E quickly.

Jess has learnt some physio exercises, on account of her going to a physio class. I have to laugh: she looks like a fly on its back, or an old lady who's fallen and can't get up.

WEEK TWENTY ONE

I've seen Bigfoot, and she's in my living room

"I hate you for doing this to me." seethes Jess, as she attempts to negotiate her now massive baby bump whilst tying her shoes. With a look of weirdly sinister glee on her face, she continues. "Sooner or later you're going to have to cut my toenails."

This, to me, is not an attractive concept. I know that some people obsess about feet, and have various fetishes; not me. Especially when considering that a woman's feet can actually swell so much during pregnancy that they go up a shoe size, and considering again that Jess was an alarming size 7 *before* she got pregnant, I'm not relishing the prospect of clipping the toenails of a hormonal beast with clown's feet. At least it means she can no longer sneak up on me, on account of the fact that I would be able to hear the 'slap-slap-slap' of her flippers as she approaches.

Think less 'Happy Feet', more 'Slappy Feet'.

Here's the science. Her feet (and sometimes legs and hands) swell because her body is holding on to too much fluid: known as oedema. It's mainly down to the extra blood circulating in her body, and the uterus putting pressure on blood vessels in her pelvis. This particularly affects her Inferior Vena Cava, an artery that travels into her lower limbs. Pressure from this slows circulation in the area, and it is this that forces water down and out through her capillaries into her feet and ankles. It's very common, between 50 and 80% of women suffering from it. It's even worse in hot weather, which makes me wonder just how much she would swell if I left her out in the midday sun; but not enough to *actually* do it. I imagine getting kicked in the nuts by an angry pregnant woman with massive feet wouldn't feel so great.

Again, a disclaimer, so you don't sue me. If your mrs gets sudden or severe swelling in her face, hands or feet, get on to your midwife or doctor; this could be a sign of a serious condition known as pre-eclampsia.

Fortunately, there are various ways in which your mrs can relieve the pain of swollen extremities (snigger). She needs to put her feet up whenever possible, or – even better – lie down on her left side. Support tights may also help, although they will automatically make her look like a crummy old pensioner. If she does opt for this method, she'll need to put them on before she gets up in the morning, to prevent blood from pooling. She can also exercise regularly, especially by walking or swimming, but nothing too heavy. Tell her these handy tips, and you'll be a hero.

Your baby is gaining weight steadily and is now about the length of a large banana. It's intestines have developed enough that it can start absorbing small amounts of sugar that have been swilling about in the amniotic fluid and gulped down by your little sprog. Up until now the spleen and liver have been responsible for producing blood cells, but now the bone marrow has also grown enough to contribute, and will continue to do so until it is the primary producer of red blood cells in the third trimester and after birth. It's pretty active, and your mrs should have felt a good few kicks by now (by the way, it would completely freak me out if I had something living inside me). You may have also been able to feel a kick or two if you've had your hand in the right place at the right time – which, ironically, is one of the reasons you became a dad in the first place. He/she wakes and sleeps at regular intervals, similar to a newborn, and this may be obvious by its movement patterns.

It also probably knows the moves to "Can't Touch This".

Bad news for your mrs, and I'd keep this one under your hat: as the baby gains weight, so will she. During the next ten weeks, she'll put on about half of the total weight gain during her entire pregnancy, so limit the Jaffa Cakes to one or two a week, despite the fact that she'll probably have a larger appetite, maybe even craving various things. If she's craving weird things like cigarette ash, coal, wood, that kind of thing (a condition known as Pica), then I strongly suggest not letting her eat that stuff because it's dangerous, but mostly because it'll taste absolutely revolting.

Oh dear. I just thoroughly offended my mrs by suggesting that she had picked up a hand towel to dry herself with after she'd got out of the shower. It wasn't a hand towel, it was a standard size towel. It just looked smaller because of how much she's grown. Whoops...

Merely an indication of the glare I received, not how my wife looks.

WEEK TWENTY TWO

Dum, dum, dum-dum, dum, dum, dum-dum

"You know those elegant, graceful women on the front of pregnancy magazines?" I say, red-faced and straining as I heave my aching wife off the sofa. "You're not one of them, are you." Cue glare.

Jess' SPD is really playing up, to the point where her back is excruciatingly painful most of the time; so far, only a warm shower can ease the pain. I swear her pelvic joints must be so loose that one day soon the baby will just fall out and hover just above the ground in some kind of *Mission: Impossible* style pose, umbilical cord pulled tight.

If you haven't already thought about names, now's a good time to start. I'm speaking from experience when I say that it can take a *long* time for both of you to agree on a name. And by agree, I mean you protest in progressively feeble tones as your mrs grinds you down with her favourite name. Stand your ground! If she does win, I suggest ensuring that when you register the name after it's born that you go on your own so you can either change the name to yours, or give it a really funny middle name which will only be revealed on his wedding day.

WEEK TWENTY THREE

Would you like a crane?

I've made an observation, and it may well be one that you have also made, especially if you share a bed with the mother of your child. You know how when you turn over in bed, it happens in one fluid motion? Well, this goes out the window for her during pregnancy, and ends up being a laborious process involving several shifts of first the legs and hips, and then the upper body. Five minutes and several odd grunts later, she's just managed to turn over, by which time she wants to be back again.

Oh, yeah: and she sounds like one of these.

We recently purchased a pregnancy pillow, which has eased a lot of the pressure on Jess' back and hips, meaning that she can sleep better and complain less. She is worried, though, about stretch marks, and eyes with concern the small white tracks running across her belly like tree branches. She has some overly-expensive cream to rub into them every day, but the fact of the matter is that it won't do anything; the stretch marks are simply too deep within the skin for cream to touch it. To cut to the chase, any stretch marks are there to stay, although they may fade over time. This may or may not be yet another unfortunate pregnancy fact that you choose to hide from your mrs to avoid wailing/stomping/beatings.

I call them 'tiger stripes', which instantly makes them awesome.

The belly button is nearing the surface on a daily basis, like a very slow submarine. It won't be long now before it pops out and stands proud of her belly like some kind of revolting little mountain.

Right now, your baby weighs about a pound, the average final baby weight being seven pounds 3 ounces – although if you're having a May baby, studies have shown that for some reason on average babies born during this month are heavier than those born in other months. It's also interesting to know that most babies are born during the summer months, as a result of people cuddling up during the previous winter and, with the addition of a bottle or two of wine and a smoochy DVD, deciding to throw caution to the wind and ferociously bump uglies.

Whilst we're talking about weights, let's give you the lowdown on roughly just how much weight your mrs will have put on by the time your baby crowns. It looks like this: the muscle layer of the uterus weighs an extra 2lb, the placenta (which, I hear, is nice on toast) weighs in at about 1.3lb. The blood volume increase and amniotic fluid gives a combined total of 8.3lb, and then there is of course the 0.9lb she'll put on in booby goodness. Finally, as some kind of insult to her womanly pride and a big middle finger to her figure, her body will lay down some fat to provide her with additional energy for things like breastfeeding, coming to about 5.5lb.

All in all, with the baby included, this comes to 24.2lb of weight your lady friend will amass during this time. On the plus side, if the unfortunate (and idiotic) occasion arises that you actually *tell* her this, you can placate her by telling her that at least 7lbs of it will be shed in just a few hours. That still won't make her happy, though, and if you're daft enough to tell her this, then you deserve to reap the consequences.

Actually, you shouldn't feel too smug about the possibility of your mrs weighing more than you by the end of her pregnancy (she can beat you hands down at wrestling, for one). Some men actually show pregnancy symptoms along with their partners, in what is known as Couvade Syndrome. The word 'couvade' means 'to hatch or brood' in French, and it basically comes down to the man having a sympathetic pregnancy, with queasiness, weight gain, loss of sexual appetite, or even labour pains. If you are experiencing this, then don't worry – soon you will give birth, probably to your own testicles, you big girl.

Your baby is about 27cm long at the moment, and is sufficiently developed to be able to feel things when he/she touches them, with fingers that boast fully formed fingerprints. If you're having a girl, the uterus and ovaries are in place; if you're having a boy, the testes have begun to descend from the pelvis into the scrotum – which, funnily enough, happened to me the other day, I think. What can I say? I'm a late developer.

The first signs of teeth are showing beneath your baby's gumline, and about 1 in 150,000 babies are born with teeth already cut. However, this is – for the majority – restricted to two or three teeth at most, so don't expect your newborn child to look at you and give you a big toothy 'Cheshire Cat-style' grin just moments after having its cord cut. If it does, please have the presence of mind to take a photo; it'll make you a rich man.

"I need a feed; prepare to be nibbled."

WEEK TWENTY FOUR

No more discharge than usual, ma'am

With the second trimester being the 'easiest' of the trimesters (I put 'easiest' in quotation marks so as to imply that none of the trimesters are particularly easy – although both you and I know that if men were the ones who got pregnant we'd breeze through it. Do you ever hear seahorses complaining?), it might be a good idea to take your partner away for a holiday, where she can relax and take her mind off the fact that in just a few short months she'll be crimping out a fully grown baby. I would take Jess away, but for the fact that it's just gone Christmas and we're absolutely skint.

This penniless situation would be less of a pain if we'd have actually received any presents this year, but if there's one thing I've learned, it's this: when you have a child, *they* get all the presents. You get nothing. Isaac's gifts from friends and family covered a vast swathe of the living room floor come Christmas morning; our presents barely covered one half of the four-seater dining table, including presents we'd bought for ourselves to make us look a little more popular.

"Mmm, socks! Thanks me."

Now is a good time, if you haven't already, to properly sit down and just plan everything out: what goes where in the nursery, how to decorate it, baby clothes, prams...you name it, it'll need doing – unless your mrs is as anal as mine, in which case she'll have already got everything planned out in meticulous detail.

Jess is really beginning to dread labour. I can't begin to empathise, but I can imagine it's like back in school, when you had an exam coming up which you were dreading but knew you had to take; except it's not an exam, it's pushing a big thing out of a little hole, in what will probably be a very painful way. Mind you, I have had some experience of this, upon recently seeing my Christmas dinner for the second time a day later.

Boxing Day: otherwise known as 'Revenge of the Turkey'

I have attempted to offer some comfort by saying that when you consider the number of hours she'll be in labour against the number of hours there have been since the beginning of time, it's really only a very small fraction and therefore won't hurt at all, especially if she scoops a palmful of Vasoline to grease things up beforehand – but, for some reason, it hasn't helped.

Now, though, is a good time to decide on a birthing plan, if you haven't got one already; and there's a particularly helpful chapter on doing just that at the end of this book, because I'm just *that* nice.

Around this time you will probably have another appointment with your midwife, in which you will go through much of the same – urine sample, blood pressure, listening to the heartbeat, etc. – all stuff  at which you are now a seasoned pro. Don't make the mistake that Jess and I did, though, which was to notice upon entering the midwife's office a photo on the wall of her particularly ugly son, and start laughing. It's bad karma. Plus, I feel guilty about laughing at other people's ugly kids in case my unborn child just so happens to have a face like the smell of gas.

What started out as a routine appointment ended in quite the opposite manner, when Jess asked about the painful Braxton Hicks she'd been having. The midwife's face visibly dropped.

"Ooh, they shouldn't be painful," she said, "and you shouldn't be having them this early on."

Now I've complained about this midwife before, and so I never completely take as truth everything she says – I know full well, for example, that Braxton Hicks contractions are common around this time *and* can be painful – but her concern still made me concerned, and stopped me from now nervously eying her ugly kid photo.

Before we'd even had much of a chance to speak, she'd rung the local hospital and ordered us down to the labour ward.

"Off to the labour ward for you," she stated abruptly, with all the motherly care and consideration of syphilis, "you might be going through premature labour."

She also had her finger in the air as she said it, demonstrated here by Hillary Clinton.

Now Jess and I don't get flapped often, and we weren't this time (we had a good idea that there was nothing to be worried about), but it still would have been nice for the midwife to seem at least vaguely concerned, even if it was obvious she was acting.

And so, half an hour later, we are sat in a delivery room in the hospital, just a few feet away from the room in which Isaac was born. I was feeling a little nauseous, either due to the memories flooding back or the vigorous strain of Norovirus that was swilling around the building. After a while a doctor came in, carried out the same checks, and pronounced that we were fine and there was nothing to worry about. She also asked a lot of questions, including "Have you had any excessive discharge?"

For some reason she was looking at me when she asked this, and so instinctively I answered with a slightly confused but very confident "no". I'm pretty sure the question wasn't aimed at me, but at least now she knows.

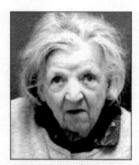

After I'd answered, her face looked like this.

Mine was like this.

WEEK TWENTY FIVE

If it starts to attack, just play dead

This week Jess booked herself a pregnancy massage using the vouchers for the local beauty place that I'd bought her for Christmas. I say 'bought her for Christmas', but in reality it was a hurried last-minute purchase on Christmas morning. You see, Jess had – like many other women – told me that this year we were going to save money and not buy for each other. I fell for this like some kind of gullible child, and was foolishly not expecting the Christmas present that was pushed into my hands on that fateful morn. Hence the laptop was opened, the debit card whipped out of my wallet and the hasty transaction made. Women, eh?

Anyway, the pregnancy massage was excellent, apparently. They raise one side of the lady with towels so arteries are not crushed by the baby, and they spend time massaging particularly painful areas. They also massage the tummy area, apparently, which sounds kind of fun. I have an image of Jess on her back, legs kicking and squirming on the massage table as the masseur tickles her stomach like an over-affectionate woman pets a puppy.

We changed midwives this week, to someone that we had during Jess' pregnancy with Isaac. She's already proven to us that she was worth it when she braved icy roads to visit Jess when she started experiencing sharp pains underneath her bump, which can be a sign of premature labour. That ex-midwife has got into our heads.

The midwife visited Jess and she took a urine test and a swab – which sounds uncomfortable yet fun. Good news is, there is no premature labour; but the midwife reckons that Jess might have an irritable uterus. I find this odd, as I would say that Jess is pretty much totally irritable right now; like a bear with a sore head, a wedgie and a couple of nasty mouth ulcers. But, if she wants to localise the irritability, that's fine with me. It turns out that Irritable Uterus has no known cause at present, and not much research has been conducted into it – but it is made worse by activities such as lifting, walking, standing, and having an orgasm. Well, we have been decorating the kitchen lately.

Premature labour is obviously a big concern for any expectant couple. If this happens then treatment will be given to slow down and (hopefully) stop the contractions. The good news is that if the baby is born now, there is around a 50% chance of survival. This increases to 80% next week, and 90% by 27 weeks. Obviously, it's best to keep it in the oven, so if your partner shows signs of premature labour (those being a contraction at least every ten minutes, watery fluid leakage, cramps, backache, bleeding) then call your midwife immediately and tell your mrs to clench.

At twenty five weeks, your baby can hear your voice, which gives you free licence to talk to your partner's bump in a ridiculous way. Just don't expect a response, and if you do get the muffly tones of a gruff "Hi, Dad" then register your child for Mensa straight away, 'cos you've spawned a genius.

Also by this week, the nostrils begin to open, the spine begins to form and the blood vessels of the lungs begin to develop – all this done under a transparent skin that is becoming more opaque every day. Time is moving along quickly, and sooner or later you're going to have to get off your bum and start to decorate the nursery. That is next on our list after we finish decorating the bedroom, although by that point I might have sawn off my own hands just so I don't have to paint another wall...twice. This would, however, make it harder to type, and punching the keyboard with my wrist stumps would probably result in pressing about five keys at once; so I might wait.

Also, keyboard rage.

Your unborn boy/girl weighs about 1.5 pounds, and is just under 9 inches long, squeezed into a uterus about the size of a football. He or she is becoming more dextrous, and can move their fingers to make a complete fist – which would explain why they are using the inside of your mrs' womb as a punchbag.

Around this time, your other half might experience itchy skin around and over her bump, caused by the stretching that it is being succumbed to. Jess is getting this, and watching her scratch it with both hands reminds me of some kind of grizzly bear. I half expect her to find the nearest tree and grind up and down it, letting out a grunt of relief every now and then.

As demonstrated.

"Which circles are clearer, the green or the red?"

"My breasts are huge." states Jess, cupping them in an action which I find rather erotic. I am inclined to agree, as I stop typing and eye her creepily over my laptop screen.

She is sat on the settee watching TV, and I'm beavering away on the computer, just waiting for the moment when I am asked to haul her to her feet so she can clump upstairs and have yet another soothing bath. Her grunts of pain as she rises from the seat have now morphed into some kind of strange breathy monkey noises; imagine Rolf Harris doing some of his weird aboriginal singing,

and you get the picture. To her credit, she hasn't let pregnancy hold her back at all, and she still works really hard for the family – which is why she often gets tired really quickly.

She has also had to resort to wearing her glasses, which she normally doesn't need as her eyesight isn't that bad. Me, I have terrible eyesight – so bad that I literally wouldn't be able to read the top letter of that illuminated sign they have at the opticians, even though I know for a fact that it is an A. It turns out that pregnancy can affect eyesight, as the same build-up of fluid that gives her unsightly cankles can affect her vision, and her hormones can also increase the thickness of the cornea on her eyeballs, blurring her sight. Fortunately, this will revert back to normal over time, and so Jess doesn't need to worry about any wrinkles caused by excessive squinting. Hopefully the cankles will make a swift exit as well...

The estimated birth date is approaching quickly, even though it feels like the pregnancy is dragging. We've not even begun to decorate the nursery yet; it's still full of old junk, like reams of books left over from the house move and a box full of tools that I don't know how to use. Now and again we'll both get really nervous of the impending labour, although I don't know why I'm that anxious, as I won't be the one pooping all over the carpet. I try to reassure her that everything will be OK by saying things like "there are some people who have like six babies, labour can't be that bad" – but it rarely has any effect other than prompting a steely glare.

Now *that* is a handful.

If you're in employment, you'll need to have told your boss by now if you're planning on taking your paternity leave. You get a choice of one or two weeks, but they have to be taken consecutively and in week chunks, not the odd day here and there. Check out the chapter at the end of this book for more info on your rights in the workplace.

Right about now, your baby – whose eyes have been closed thus far – will open them and begin to blink, revealing blue or brown eyes (depending on your ethnicity), although the colour may change after birth. What it'll make of its accommodation is anyone's guess, but I can imagine what'd be going through my mind if I was balled up in a sphere of flesh and goo. There would be one strongly worded letter to management being sent that day.

"And the walls were FILTHY!"

He or she weighs around 2 pounds and measures just over 9 inches, which means it'll certainly be able to make itself known as it boots your mrs' insides. Although it will have been used to noises for weeks now, such as your partner's heartbeat or the sounds of her digestive system, she may find that it jumps on loud noises. It can also tell if it is light or dark outside – the walls of the uterus are so stretched that some light can get through.

Oh, and by the way, it's happened. Her belly button is now most definitely an outie and seems to be pointing at me no matter where I'm standing in the room, like a gross little finger or Mona Lisa's eyes. Despite this, I can't seem to stop pressing it like a button, although I'm not sure what I'm expecting to happen.

Oops...

WEEK TWENTY SEVEN

Iron in, as opposed to ironing

I know I'm not the one giving birth, but I still regard the impending due date with a bit of anxiety and (dare I say it) fear. Sure, it'll be easy for me; the hardest thing I'll have to do is use a net to pluck a turd from the grimy waters of a bath, if we use one – but as any partner will know, they do not like to see their loved one in pain. To counteract this, and minimise any potential stress, good preparation is vital. Check out the chapters at the end of this book for some advice on getting ready for the big day.

Swiss Army Knife probably not required, although still awesome.

Here's something about me: I'm stingy. I hate spending if I don't have to, hence the pathetic wedge cushion I bought Jess a few weeks ago which has served only as a good weapon to beat me with when I say something sarcastic about her. However, I've given in and shelled out the cash on an all-singing, all-dancing maternity cushion that goes up between her legs, under her head, probably everywhere a cushion could go. I'd have thought that she was used to having something big and comfortable between her legs every night. It turns out: no.

I hope it works, though; seeing Jess scooching down the stairs on her bum because her back hurts is awesomely funny to watch, but can't be a barrel of laughs for her.

Like a slinky, only about 10% as grateful.

We had a midwife appointment this week, in which they took some more blood from Jess to check for various things – one of them being anaemia. It turns out that Jess is anaemic, which would explain the general paleness and tiredness, and as a result she's been put on iron tablets – which, she tells me ever so matter-of-factly, make her poo jet black. This, she says, makes her feel like a devil woman. I'm inclined to agree.

It also turns out that the baby is breech, which means instead of lying head down, it's instead lying in a rather more head up position. To help fix this, Jess has been advised that she should sit with her knees below her hips, and do plenty of exercise. If none of this works, then the next step is acupuncture – which, with Jess' inherent fear of needles, is probably a bad road to go down. The only other option is the baby being manually turned by a doctor, which I'm told hurts a lot; so here's hoping the exercise works...

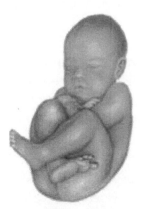

"CANNONBALL!!"

According to the midwife, swimming is the best form of exercise, as it takes pressure off aching joints. Therefore, Jess has deemed it fit to drag me to the local pool once a week to go up and down, up and down, doing what I think is breast stroke but which is more likely to be a mixture of doggy paddle and panicked flailing. I'm an alright swimmer, and it's not the swimming itself that I don't like, it's the stuff that comes with it. I hate the revolting nature of the changing room floors, I hate the fact that the lockers are always too small for your clothes, and I *detest* the fact that every other man in the changing rooms has no modicum of modesty, instead insisting on dangling their giblets in your face with not even a half-hearted attempt to cover themselves up. I do love, however, the funky machine that gets your shorts dry really quickly.

Your baby is now about 35cm long from head to bum, which is pretty impressive. Watching Jess' bump move around as my baby does is both fascinating and incredibly freaky. Gestation is weird, man.

The retinas of your baby are continuing to form, and its eyes open more often. Its brain, liver and immune systems are still developing, but your child will still stand a great chance of survival if born right now.

Some experts believe that babies begin to dream around this time. How they can tell that, I don't know, but I can't imagine that the baby dreams about much anyway. It's not like it's watched *Saving Private Ryan* a few hours earlier and will dream about storming the Normandy beaches. They must just dream about floating around in a cramped ball of fluid, then wake up and think "Aww, man, it's real life as well! How dull!"

Your mrs may find herself short of breath, as the uterus is now up near her rib cage. This is expected, and does not harm the baby – in fact, thanks to all the pregnancy hormones swilling around in your partner's blood, the circulatory system actually works more effectively.

Awesome fact: the average breast weighs about seven ounces, and during pregnancy can double. That's just one breast. Your partner has two. How do they ever get anything done?!

WEEK TWENTY EIGHT

I admit it: being a woman must suck

I have a wisdom tooth growing through and the pressure on my gum is causing untold pain.

"You have no idea how much pain I'm in." I mutter glumly, nursing my jaw. Cue a stare that would make a nun cry.

I said "cry", but I forgive you, because you're old and energetic.

I suppose it is a tad unfair, this whole pregnancy thing. My part lasts – and I quote my beloved wife – "90 seconds", whilst she has to endure discomfort, aches and the odd bout of diarrhoea for nine months, which culminates in potentially hours of excruciating pain. Then, there will be further pain whilst breastfeeding, not to mention stitches, mastitis and the threat of post-natal depression. Oh, and there'll be a baby to look after.

As I try to avoid the Medusa-like glower of my beautiful wife and take a long hard think about what I've done, I can't help but feel ongoing and immense sympathy for what she is going through without, to be fair, excessive whinging. She could easily have stayed in bed most days, like back in the medieval era, but instead she has remained active and always put Isaac first, and so for that I give a hearty applause. Well, I would – but I seem to be frozen with fear.

That's not to say that I still don't find some of her discomfort and cumbersomeness rather entertaining, in a vaguely mean kind of way. For example, the big fancy maternity pillow came this week, and whenever I see Jess turning over in bed grappling this ridiculously large thing, I can't help but think of the late great Steve Irwin wrestling crocodiles. I realise that sounds a bit insensitive and I do sympathise, but don't judge me: you laugh when children and old people fall down, I bet.

Your mrs is now in the third trimester, which means she's more or less on the home straight. Your baby is composed of around 2 to 3% body fat, which is pretty much what I was like before I got married and didn't have to keep trying to impress. The lungs are capable of breathing air now, but if premature labour meant you met your little one early, it would still struggle to breathe without the aid of medical equipment. He or she can now recognise your voice, so the more you talk to it, the better. Their eyebrows continue to grow, hopefully independently, thus avoiding a rather revolting monobrow situation, although that would be kind of cool.

"Hola! Eez time for nappy change, no?"

WEEK TWENTY NINE

All she needs now are the tiny little arms

You know when you're sat on the loo after a particularly challenging steak the night before, and you know it's going to be a big one, yet you also know that it is inevitable that somehow, at some point, it has to come out, and if it stays in there it's only going to get bigger? After hours of semi-careful thought, that is the best way that I can think of to describe how Jess must be feeling just a few weeks before the big day. I mean of course, don't get me wrong; I've never known anyone spend 36 hours doing a poo, and I'd like to think that I eat just enough fruit to avoid tearing my perineum wide open, but with my vulgar man's brain it's the best I can come up with.

As I smirk to myself whilst watching Jess hobble across the living room floor (her back is quite bad today, and so she's walking like a T-Rex with a broom up it's bum), I can't help but feel sorry for what she will have to go through soon. Of course, I'll be there with her every step of the way, but at the end of the day it won't be me squatting on the floor ankle deep in weird fluids. This pang of sympathy prompts me to think about making a cup of tea. I don't. I'm too busy writing this.

Jess seems to be having a recurrence of the symptoms that you would only normally see in early pregnancy: nausea, vomiting, nose bleeds. At least, I'd like to think that this is what's happening, and that these conditions are not as a direct result of marriage to me. It's all very strange; however, at this point, both you and I have become somewhat immune to the oddities that pregnancy brings. I mean, get this: the other day Jess cried when I asked her if she wanted green tea or normal tea. The decision was literally so mind-blowingly great that it prompted her to burst into tears and sob for a good couple of minutes. Whereas a few months ago I would have been incredibly bemused, I now dispense a few consoling hugs, a peck on the forehead, and attempt to actually get the answer out of her.

"YOU'RE HAVING GREEN!" "NO, I DON'T WANT GREEN!
...Actually, yeah, I do want green."

You may be going to antenatal classes around this time - which can be really helpful, dependant upon the midwife leading the group. I remember one class (when we were pregnant with Isaac) where the midwife made all the dads stand up and rock an imaginary baby. Did I learn a lot? Heck yes. I learnt that standing up with a lot of confused and slightly embarrassed men and gently swaying from side to side teaches you very little about childbirth and babies, instead serving only to make you look like a plonker.

By now, your baby (weighing just over a kilo) should be merrily moving around in the uterus it calls home, giving the occasional uppercut or Jean Claude Van Damme-style martial arts kick to your mrs' internal organs. It is good every now and then for your partner to keep a mental check on your baby's movements; they say that if it moves fewer than ten times a day, ring your midwife and let them know. It could be something, it could be nothing. I'm a fully grown male with a desk job; I barely move ten times in a week.

As well as punching like Jackie Chan, your foetus is probably about the same size as him.

Fortunately, your child's head is now in proportion to the rest of it's body, which means it'll avoid unnecessary and rather mean teasing at school (I'll never forget old 'bobblehead' in Year Six). The brain can now control primitive breathing and body temperature, and the eyes can look around a bit more. The bone marrow is also now completely in charge of red blood cell production, and your baby is also urinating about half a litre of pee into the amniotic fluid every day, which can't be pleasant for anyone but has to be done.

Your baby can also sense light, and will turn towards it. This doesn't mean, however, that you can try and freak out your unborn child by wildly flashing a torch at your mrs' belly. It won't work, and is rather mean.

WEEK THIRTY

Where money from the government can buy clothes and video games

"Thirty two weeks today," beams Jess, her cheeks flushed after a particularly exerting trip up the stairs. "We're getting close."

I feel bad, like you do when you're about to tell a child that his pet dog has been violently run over by a couple of cars.

"Umm, actually," I begin, raising my hands to my chin in a boxer-style attempt to parry any blows that might come my way, "You're only thirty weeks."

"Not the face!"

Jess pauses and gazes into the middle distance, counting out weeks on her fingers, which are now so swollen she can no longer wear her wedding and engagement rings. After a few seconds, the thoughtful gaze drops and is replaced by a glare that indicates she hates the world and everything in it.

"Oh yeah. Well that sucks." she grumbles, and continues glossing the skirting boards in the nursery. I snigger to myself and carry on typing. I should add at this point that Jess *wanted* to gloss, and I've not forced her into any kind of manual labour. The nursery is coming along nicely, although we've not yet got round to buying any clothes for the newborn; so if he decides to come early we're just going to have to swaddle him in toilet roll and a bit of old carpet for the time being.

Around this time, you and your partner can apply for the Sure Start Maternity Grant (in the UK), if you meet certain criteria. It's a one-off cash sum of up to £500, which would probably cover the cost of your average ladies' haircut. I jest: we don't qualify for this grant, though, but we do automatically get a Health in Pregnancy Grant of £190, and when we get it, it's going towards a new cot, a pram, and an Xbox. But probably not the Xbox.

But almost definitely the Xbox.

Right now, your baby is practising breathing by repeatedly moving the diaphragm. This can often lead to hiccups, which feel like rhythmic twitches in the uterus, so I'm told. It weighs around three pounds, and measures around 14 to 15 inches from crown to rump ('rump' is one of my all-time favourite words. Say it out loud, go on. Funny, isn't it?). It's lungs and digestive system is almost fully developed, and your baby is gaining weight steadily. Hopefully, if your partner is one of the lucky ones, it'll be head down and firmly lodged in position by now; if not, there are various exercises your mrs can do in order to rotate it.

I look up as I write this, and Jess is attempting to prise herself from the sofa. *Look at her*, I think, and smile to myself. *She's glowing.* My face drops. *No, wait: glowering.*

WEEK THIRTY ONE

Break out the earplugs, it's going to get loud

I made the mistake the other day of watching a television programme in which they showed childbirth, and now I'm freaking out. Well - I'm quite a laid back person, so 'freaking out' for me consists more of sitting rigidly still and staring wide-eyed at the wall with a runny nose in some kind of Blair Witch-style pose, than running around screaming and gnawing on the edge of the sofa. I'll be honest, though, I think I dilated 8 centimetres just watching it.

"I can feel my waters bulging…"

It's not so much the close-up and rather graphic shots of the head and shoulders of a gooey child hanging upside-down that bother me, although I have made a silent mental note to *not* go down the business end when Jess gives birth. It's more this: women, I have noticed, tend to make a lot of noise during labour. Some groan like a rutting stag, some blare out a constant sound steadily rising in pitch like a World War Two air raid siren, and some just scream like they're on a roller coaster. I have sympathy up to a point, but the other day I did a dump which was at least 7lb 8oz with no more than a slight grunt and a couple of rosy cheeks.

"WHAT DO YOU MEAN THE HEAD'S NOT EVEN OUT YET?!"

To Jess' credit, when she gave birth to Isaac she barely made any sound at all, at least none I could hear over the sound of my own panicked wails. Every time is different, though, and especially with us having a home birth I'm concerned that the unfortunate neighbours on the other side of the thin wall that separates our houses might think there's some kind of gruesome murder going on and call the police. Plus, I am definitely unprepared for a home birth at the moment. If my sprog were to arrive now, his first contact would be the soggy side of a shower curtain. Or a well-placed baseball glove.

Not that there's much chance of him coming out yet, and Jess is becoming increasingly fed up. He's still breech, and refusing to budge, despite her strange rocking on all fours which supposedly helps him turn. We had another appointment this week, in which the midwife suggested we try some strange thing called moxibustion.

Nothing like spontaneous combustion.

From what I can gather after Googling the heck out of this strange procedure is that moxibustion involves burning a small spongy herb named Mugwort on acupuncture needles, in a technique which originated in China – where most strange things come from. It's meant to stimulate blood flow and whatnot, and sounds like complete bunkum to me, but we're prepared to try whatever to get the little git to turn over. According to the *Journal of the American Medical Association*, an experiment showed that up to 75% of women suffering from breech presentations before childbirth had foetuses that rotated to the normal position after undergoing moxibustion. Sounds to me like an excuse for Jess to get high 'Chinese-style', but there you go. I've learnt not to try and argue with her, because she's bigger than me now and could probably cause some serious physical damage. It'd be like that bit in *Jurassic Park* where the T-Rex is chasing the jeep, and I wouldn't put it past her to bite my head off as I sit on the toilet.

WEEK THIRTY TWO

"He just slipped out, honest."

This week we attended an antenatal home birth class down at some Quaker centre in the local town. Jess had concerns about being the largest pregnant woman there, and rightly so. She's swelled somewhat lately.

Was it a helpful class? Kinda. Was it full of hippies? Umm, yeah. We began by all sitting in a big circle as one or two recent new mums recounted their wonderful birth stories about how easy it was, how little Timmy just slid out, how that the whole house was serene and calm. You could see all the expectant parents drinking this in, and I don't know if it was because I was in a Quaker centre with no sign of porridge, or because I had to pay £2 just to park at the damn place, but I felt like sticking my hand up and stating "Err, yeah, when Jess had our first one there was gunk everywhere and she did a poo on the floor." That'd shut them up.

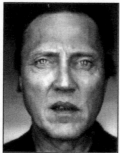

Yeah, I know this is Christopher Walken, but it's a good indication of how their faces would have looked.

I didn't do that though; the thought of dozens of angry women glaring at me and then slowly advancing as I back into the corner put me off opening my mouth. I did ask loads of questions, and to be fair we both came away from the class feeling much more positive about having a home birth. I'm sure there were lots of other interesting things said, but one woman decided to breastfeed halfway through the class, and so I spent the rest of my time trying to subtly crane my neck to see if I could catch a glimpse of nip.

I sound like I'm being harsh to all the softly spoken midwives, mothers who have had five kids yet still come back for more, and clearly terrified new parents who spent the whole class practically rocking back and forth on the floor in something resembling the foetal position (ironically). It  gave a good insight into how home births work, and people could exchange tips on how to keep nosey visitors from knocking on your door at all hours; although my suggestion of sticking a rifle through the letterbox and firing at random didn't go down well. No-one also got the joke when I told them I'd already bought a carpet cleaner in preparation for the birth. They just stared me up and down then carried on talking about doulas. Mental note: if I was to ever become a radio presenter or club musician, DJ Doula would be an awesome title.

Later that evening, Jess started feeling very faint and sick, symptoms which culminated at about 1am with her blowing chunks into a strategically placed bucket. Listening to someone be sick has to be one of the most revolting sounds ever, especially as Jess doesn't hold back with the feminine grace that many other women have. When she voms, she voms with vigour. Of course, it's down to yours truly to dispose of the puke; cue me running across the landing, holding a bin at arms length and breathing through my mouth.

In the depths of your partner's bulging abdomen, the final touches are being placed on your baby. Eyelashes, eyebrows and head hair are evident; pubic hair, however, comes much later, and would look weird on a baby. The lanugo hair that has covered your baby for a couple of months is beginning to shed. Although his or her lungs aren't yet fully developed, it will still have a fantastic chance of survival if born now. At the moment, it is inhaling amniotic fluid in order to exercise it's lungs and get some practice in.

If your mrs has trouble with bad circulation in her legs, she might want to think about some maternity support tights. As if she isn't sexy enough already…

WEEK THIRTY THREE
I'll fetch the oil

"Perineal massage is a way of preparing the tissues of the perineum for the stretching that is necessary during childbirth." reads my wife, her face illuminated by the glow from the laptop. I stop picking my toenails and look up, nose wrinkled. For some reason, she reads on.

"Prepare yourself mentally for sticking your thumbs inside yourself." she continues, as I dry retch over the carpet. "Advanced students of perineal massage may prefer to get their partners to massage the perineum as an opportunity to share intimacy -"

"Whoa, stop right there!" I cry, my hands raised, palms out. "I ain't going anywhere *near* your perineum!"

Not without a full hazard suit.

Jess laughs – well, guffaws – and I get over the rising nausea enough to do the same. Of course, we have an open mind when it comes to childbirth preparations, but I'd rather spoon a tramp than start prodding around my wife's perineum.

Jess had a midwife appointment this week, in which – after much very painful looking pinching and groping – the midwife told her that our baby had got his act together, done a triple somersault double pike, turned upside down and was beginning to engage (which conjures up images of either a capsule docking with a space station, or a puppy getting it's head stuck in a drainpipe). This is known as 'cephalic'. Write that down, and amaze your mrs with it later. Just casually drop it  into conversation, like "Hey, our baby is like, SO cephalic right now..." and just watch her gawp at you as you nod to yourself smugly.

The midwife also casually dropped into conversation that the baby already weighs six pounds. This understandably came as a shock to Jess; I remained characteristically cool. If Jess were to go full term, the graph in our notes tells us that our baby would be a whopping ten pound lump of flesh, with just a head and limbs to distinguish it from a large piece of ham. Outwardly, upon hearing this news, I extended sympathy; inside, I was giving little celebratory fist-pumps that I was not the poor person who had to squeeze that one out.

Like pushing a watermelon through a drainpipe.

Your baby's brain is rapidly developing this week, inside a skull made of soft bones that won't fuse completely for a good couple of years, giving you an awful lot of time to practice the art of self-restraint as that niggling voice in your head urges you to press the soft spot to see what happens. (Please don't. My family spent so much time poking my brain through my scalp that I can't remember the second half of the alphabet, and my skull bones only joined together last week.) His or her lungs are now pretty much fully developed, so much so that if your mrs was to go into labour now, there would be minimal outside assistance needed.

This news that the baby might be pooing all over my hand in as little as three weeks has prompted us to get the hospital bag ready (just in case), as well as get stuff together in preparation for the home birth. There's a few chapters at the end of this sterling read to guide you through what stuff to get packed, although if your mrs is anything like mine, she's already done it.

Jess has got me oiling up and massaging her grossly swollen feet, which reminds me of marinating a couple of massive chicken breasts. She also sent me out the other night to fetch her a cheeseburger. Once again, her cravings just so happen to be delicious. Funny, that!

Although she has a point.

WEEK THIRTY FOUR
If you ask me that question once more, I swear I'll cry

"So how long have you got left?"
"Are you sure there's not two in there? They hide behind each other on scans, you know."
(Upon hearing the response to the first question, with a look of polite shock as they regard the sheer size of your partner) "Oh…wow…" Rough translation: Man, you're huge.

There may be variants to this theme; but after hearing the same questions asked week in week out by the same people who think they're cracking the joke for the first time, I think it should be perfectly acceptable (and legal) to plant the sweetest of roundhouse kicks onto their lower jaw.

Seriously, you'll have noticed this by now: the same questions, again and again, often coupled with sundry belly touchings. Now, I know, they're not touching my belly, although the odd tickle now and again would be nice; but you have to feel for your poor mrs as, once again and through a gritted smile, she gives the same response to the same question for the sixtieth time.

This week we had an additional ultrasound to check the position of the baby, due to the fact that we're having a home birth. I have to express, at this point, my admiration for sonographers everywhere; how on earth they can make out anything in that swirling mass of grey is beyond me. This is more applicable, perhaps, in the early scans; in the later ones, such as the one we had today, even I could make stuff out, and I'm short-sighted. The most surreal part was the ultra-clear image we got of our baby's face, which was pretty freaky. Not the face, I should add, but the experience; although, with a father like me, the poor beggar doesn't stand much of a chance.

My bad.

The lanugo hair on your baby's skin is now continuing to come off, and the vernix coating is becoming thicker: a greasy white substance that moisturises the baby's skin (although Oil of Olay probably smells nicer), and allows a smoother passage through the birth canal. Imagine trying to grab onto a wet bar of soap, and you get the idea. Your baby is also urinating about a pint a day, which is pretty good going, considering that on a particularly hot day the best I can manage is a dribble that has the colour and consistency of honey (I'm not a big drinker). It weighs about four and a half pounds, and measures approximately 18 inches long from head to toe. If he or she was to come out now, it would be classed as a 'pre-term' labour instead of a 'premature', a 'pre-term' baby less likely to require intensive care treatment, due to a 95-99% survival rate. We're on the final straight now, and your baby is getting ready to enter the world from the gooey cosiness of your partner's womb.

I, on the other hand, continue my banishment from the bed, as Jess claims she 'needs the space'. Sleeping on the settee isn't that uncomfortable, I suppose, if you ignore the biting cold, itchy fabric and the fact that cushions are no good at spooning.

Although 'girlfriend pillows' exist. Hey, I'm not judging. (Loners)

WEEK THIRTY FIVE

Don't blame me, blame alcohol

"I hate your sperm." scowls my glowing wife, eyeing me across the dinner table. She looks like she's ready to pounce, like a huge cumbersome tiger.

There's not a lot I can say in response to that, other than offer twenty million apologies; fifty million on a good day. The poor little guys get no credit. Although, how awesome would you feel if you were the one sperm out of twenty million that managed to fertilise the egg? You'd have to do some kind of strange spermy victory dance, that's for sure. 'Sperm'. Funny word.

Jess is actually beginning to resent me a bit. I know! Me, of all people! I've been nothing but charming. It's because she wants to be skinny and fit. I'm neither, having recently grown a second chin and often hyperventilating during the walk from the house to my car; but I'm still skinnier and fitter than her, and so I'm on her black list. I probably don't help matters: it really annoys her when I overtake her on the stairs.

Jess is also going through panty-liners like they're going out of fashion, although I'm not sure they were ever *in* fashion. This is on account of increased cervical mucous production, which is common at this stage. She also suffers a lot with pins and needles in her toes and hands – which are swelling by the day, making her look like the Michelin Man. Cervical mucous, pins, and needles: the ingredients of possibly the worst recipe ever.

This week sees your baby's most rapid period of weight gain, rising from around 5 and a half pounds by another eight to twelve ounces. Because of this, the child is getting mega cramped, which may result in decreased movements – although when it does move, it'll be stronger and more forceful as the baby goes all Bruce Lee on your partner's abs. Our sprog is keeping Jess up all night, which is causing her to lose sleep and feel a bit grotty. I'm still on the sofa, which is actually getting pretty comfortable now, if you don't mind waking up with your neck bent out of shape.

WEEK THIRTY SIX

Houston, we are engaged and ready for launch

This week began by a trip to the hospital. Jess' hands and feet had swelled so much her toes looked like they warranted their own biceps, and as well as this she was feeling really ill. I rang the local hospital for advice, and they told us to go down to get it checked out, and so we did.

Fifteen minutes later we were in the labour ward, Jess hooked up to a machine where we could hear the hoofbeat sounds of our baby's heartbeat as the corridors echoed with the faint wails and beastly screams of women in labour, punctuated by the squeaky cry of a newborn. Fortunately, everything's fine, and after twenty minutes of lying around as woman after sweaty, flushed woman was wheeled past proudly clutching a baby, we were allowed to go.

She has been having contractions now and then, though; only short ones, and they fade away after a few minutes, but it seems now that the arrival of our boy won't be far away. He's five-fifths engaged, which is pretty much the most engaged one baby can be, so any day now I'm expecting a text or phone call informing me of a bloody show – which has nothing to do with expressing disgust at a poor performance of Cats. I'm not really excited, but I don't mean that in a bad way; at the moment I'm more nervous. The excitement and erratic whooping will come once I know that both mum and baby are safe and sound. Until then, I'll just keep clenching the ol' pelvic floors and hope that I don't wet myself with anxious pee.

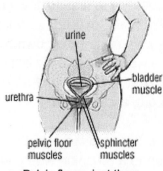

Pelvic floors, just there.

Jess is getting seriously fed up, though, and is incredibly uncomfortable. She just wants him out, and is at the point where she is about to try anything to do so: you know the usual things, pineapple, long walks, and so on. She's stopped short at sex though, and I have the feeling that she's so uncomfortable she's more likely to seek a kick-start from a certain Mr Rogan Josh before she turns to me – who she now regards as 'the tool who got me in this situation in the first place'.

Your foetus (probably not the most affectionate term, but we'll roll with it) has now put on a few pounds, and is beginning to sport a pair of chubby face cheeks that will get pinched incessantly shortly after birth by a stereotypical plump relative that you undoubtedly have. The bones in its skull have now fully formed, but have not joined together. Instead, they move and flex to allow for an easier birth. I wish I was the one adult whose skull bones never fused. I'd freak old people out by squeezing my head through their letterbox.

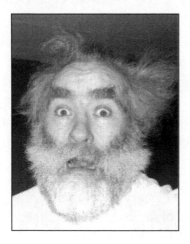

WEEK THIRTY SEVEN

Not that I ever massage children, mind you

Mental note: apparently, "Sucks to be you" is not an acceptable response after your mrs grumbles about how uncomfortable she is. You may feel I'm being harsh, and I probably am; but I've been massaging her feet for about fifteen minutes now, and they're so large it's akin to rubbing suncream into a child's back.

Mind you, I can't compare the disgusting wrinkledness of my overly-moisturised hands to her discomfort. She desperately wants the baby out now; she's in almost constant pain with her SPD, and keeps getting the odd contraction, but it never leads to anything. She went for a professional reflexology massage the other day (which I don't suppose was half as good as my haphazard thumb-rubbings) which can stimulate contractions and labour, and it won't be long before she's face-deep in a pineapple whilst going on a long walk.

It's doubtful she'd look this happy.

You'll be aware that some babies are born with a full head of hair, and at this stage it can be almost four centimetres long. I'm sure you – like me – are hoping that the hair is limited to his scalp area only, and that your baby doesn't come out looking like the Wolf Man or the Bearded Lady; although you would get a few quid from the local media. Also, if your baby had corn rows or dreadlocks, that'd be cool.

The vernix caseosa and lanugo is pretty much gone, swallowed by your baby, who weighs about six pounds and measures 14 inches, crown to rump (21 inches overall). It's getting ready to come out, so if you haven't already, get your hospital bag packed; sometime soon you're going to get that text, phone call or nudge in the side from your mrs to say it's all kicking off, and you don't want to be left running around like a nutcase as her waters break all over your nice tile floor.

WEEK THIRTY EIGHT
My lovely lady trumps

I've learned to keep my mouth shut, as it always seems to get me in some kind of trouble - or at the very least earns me a withering stare. My suggestion of putting a rusk at the entrance to her lady parts to try and coax the child out met with a snigger, which made her back hurt, and so the smile quickly turned to pursed lips.

That's right – still no baby, and Jess is getting mega grumpy. I'm going to take the advice of one Mr Ronan Keating, who wisely sang "you say it best when you say nothing at all". I'm not going to take his further advice of "life is a roller coaster, just gotta ride it"; I'm not a big fan of roller coasters, purely because that photo they take of you just as you're in the throes of being pulled around by various G-forces is never very flattering. I'm fed up of assembling at the booth where they display your

photo on TV screens and hearing old women say "Ah, bless. It's nice that they let the simple ones on the rides."

Jess has also started farting a lot in her sleep, which is one of the few things that makes me grateful I'm still relegated to the sofa. The trumps aren't particularly loud, or particularly quiet; they're just ones that sound like the noise kids make when they're blowing bubbles with their own spit.

We had another midwife appointment this week,  who found that our foetus was 1/5 palpable, which basically means that when she pinches and squeezes Jess 'down there' she can feel about 1/5 of his head – so he's 4/5 engaged, which is 1/5 less than last week, which I suppose is a bad thing, I'm not that sure. I just blew my own mind with all those fractions.

Your baby could be gaining as much as one ounce a day in weight at the moment, a fact which will probably fill your partner with a sense of dread and urgency as she ponders the prospect of having to push a little bit more. All that lanugo and amniotic fluid your baby has eaten is going to shoot out in your baby's first poo, known medically as meconium; a greenish-black liquid that is pretty revolting. I just thought you should know, so you can keep an eye out for it: Isaac decided to spray his all over my arm, and for some reason I didn't notice until I wiped my forehead and wondered why the midwives began to heave.

WEEK THIRTY NINE AND SIX DAYS
Knock knock. Who's there? BABY

It was about 2am when Jess rudely decided to start with the contractions, meaning that I had had a grand total of one hour's sleep. Yes, I know, I shouldn't have gone to bed so late, but can we focus here? I'm trying to tell you the birth story!

That's right – our little boy is finally here. As Jess woke me up, I muttered something incoherent in a somewhat groggy state and hauled myself off the settee, by which point Jess was doing a wee and contracting at the same time, something of a feat – although anyone who's ever sat on a freezing cold toilet seat would be able to tell you a thing or two about contracting and peeing simultaneously.

We'd rehearsed this scenario many times, and so – like some kind of ridiculously skinny commando – I get to work putting into action Operation Emerging Slimey, taking the box of shower curtains and old towels downstairs in preparation for the various bodily fluids that would be flung around the living room.

I make a note of the time of each contraction and how long it lasts. I can tell when Jess is having one of these tightenings as she pulls what only be described as her 'contraction face'. An unimaginative title, I know, but each woman has that facial expression that they only pull as their uterus tightens during the throes of labour. Jess' looks like someone has punched her right in the nose, her eyes squeezed shut and mouth in a pursed 'O'. Basically, if it were an emoticon, it'd be XO.

The contractions get to about five minutes apart, and so I ring the hospital to request that the midwife come out, and we can get cracking with the home birth. However, it seems we have picked the one day of the year that all on-call midwives are off sick; bad news for Jess, as she had her heart set on a home birth. Despite this upset, however, I am not trained to deliver a child on my own, no matter how helpful YouTube might be, and so we call my mother-in-law and ask her to come over to babysit Isaac when he wakes up whilst we go to the hospital.

We throw the hospital bags into the car and make our way on a tank of petrol that is far lower than it should be, but hey, I'm a 25 year-old with two kids, I live on the edge. Take note: you never realise how bumpy roads can be until your partner is yelping as you pass over each tiny pothole, or wheezing as she is pressed against the window as you career around corners.

We arrive at the hospital, and eventually get to the labour ward, stopping every few steps so Jess can prop herself against a wall and carry out some heavy breathing whilst 'XO'ing vehemently. The labour ward is packed, but we are given a bed across the ward from a woman who – judging by the ever-increasing pitches of her contraction-induced moans – is nearing the end. Eventually we collar a midwife for long enough to stick the TENS machine pads on Jess' back, and she foolishly puts me in charge of the strength of the electric pulse. Needless to say, it takes a bit of trial and error to find a happy medium, although it is kind of funny to watch Jess flap at me as I zap the living heck out of her back.

Spasming like a fish out of water.

This continues for just over an hour, and I catch the odd midwife eyeing me disapprovingly as I stand an arm's length away from Jess as she pulls contraction faces and grips onto the sheets. I can understand; to the neutral observer, I must just look like I'm not caring. But I know full well that any kind of bodily contact, even a hand-hold, is not permitted when Jess is in pain, and would result in a fist swung my way.

Eventually, a midwife enters through the flimsy curtains, and we get Jess onto her back for the vaginal exam. I know I'm making it sound like we're manoeuvring a beached whale, but it's 4 in the morning and Jess is knackered, as well as being in a lot of pain; but nothing like the pain that she is in when the midwife starts using all of her fingers to poke and prod around her special region; I have the fingernail marks on the back of my hand to prove it. That's right: the only time she wants to hold my hand is when she's tearing it to shreds with nails that I can only assume have been filed to a point especially for the occasion.

Nursing the back of my hand, and trying not to well up – it's only fairly certain that Jess is in more pain than I am, after all, and I don't want to look like a baby – the midwife finishes her brutal act and declares that 'there's no cervix left, and it's just the waters holding him back'. Man, that was fast. In the space of about two hours Jess has gone from 0-10cm dilation, like the cervical version of a Ferrari, and now the reality of the situation is beginning to sink in for me. A little late, I know, but suddenly I realise I'm going to be a dad again. I don't do anything melodramatic, like pass out or vomit everywhere – just a few deep breaths and gritted teeth, on account of the claws still digging into my hand.

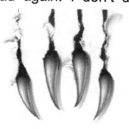

Because she is finding it difficult to move, we wheel Jess into one of the delivery rooms on the bed, whack on a fan to keep her cool, and play the waiting game for her waters to burst. This takes about an hour, at one point both myself and the midwife sat side-by-side, chin in hands, just watching Jess 'XO' as if she's some kind of terrible hospital drama. Finally, we convince her to kneel on all fours, and it's not long before the moan, accompanied by the pop, accompanied by the sound of splashing fluids - like the sound you get when someone throws a water balloon against a brick wall - indicates quite strongly that her waters have broken.

There's meconium in the waters, which means that our boy's decided to take a dump whilst still in the womb; a terribly filthy idea. There's no immediate risk to the baby, though, and the midwife simply takes precautions by listening to his heartbeat more regularly.

Then, boom. We're into the pushing; Jess' hips heaving down, once or twice every few minutes. She's being very good, sound-wise: the only sound passing through lips and gritted teeth being some kind of angry, caveman, throaty anguish, gently rising in pitch and volume until the push is over. I keep myself firmly away from the business end, and the reasons are two-fold: firstly, I've caught a glimpse of the various bodily fluids coating the mattress, and I have no intentions of seeing more. Secondly, if I did, it is likely that my face would be torn off by Jess' teeth. Oh, there's a third – who would want to see that? 'But it's a wonderful occurrence, crowning!' I hear you cry, and in part I agree; but anyone who voluntarily risks having the image of his wife's woo-woo looking like the daggy end of a sheep burnt into his memory for life is mad, in my opinion.

5.37am, and the head is out, the baby looking around from the neck up, like an unwell woman wrapped up in a duvet. One more push, and one minute later, and the rest of our boy slides out amidst one final stifled groan from his mum. He begins crying straight away, which is the sound that I most wanted to hear after watching all of those scare-mongering programmes a few weeks ago where the baby doesn't breathe for ages. He's towelled off, and I cut the cord – which is like scissoring through gammon - as Jess grows teary in a mixture of relief and joy. And yes, I'm welling up. Not so much as to have any tears running down my cheeks, but enough to look glassy-eyed and purse-lipped as I hold back from blubbering.

Scalp still bloodied from a tear that Jess sustained, and with a bit of gross goo in the corner of his eyes, little Noah William is placed into Jess' arms, and I kiss her forehead and tell her how proud I am of her as I gaze upon my foetus-turned-baby.

I'm going to shock you here with something that is rarely spoken out loud but is often true: newborn babies are ugly. Of course, at the time, you think they're gorgeous; and as I look at Noah now, asleep in his Moses basket, I wouldn't describe him in any other way; but give it a few months, and we'll look back at the photos of him barely a few minutes old, and think about how much he looks like a shrivelled old man. It's just something I thought I should put out there. Sorry.

The placenta is passed after a painful injection into Jess' thigh, and the midwife sets to work stitching her up – which, judging by the high-pitched cries of "ow-ow-OW!" - is more painful than the birth itself. I stand and gently rock Noah, pacing around the humid and stuffy delivery room, bobbing him up and down and looking at how beautiful his little mouth is, and the fingers that he gropes at his face with, and trying to ignore the continual throbbing pain of the fingernail marks that plague the majority of my hand.

Soon, he does his first (or is it second?) poo, a thick, black, tar-like substance that takes forever to wipe off his skin. Whilst changing his nappy, I notice that his ball bags are huge, something which is common in baby boys (not so much in the girls). I should state, my son does not have snooker-ball sized testicles; it's simply fluid retention. If it was the testicles thing, I'd be dead jealous.

There's not a lot else to report: Noah is weighed (a beefy 8lb 10.5oz), dressed, and little tags wrapped around his ankles. We're fortunate enough to be able to go home a few hours later, once I've driven back to the house to pick up the car seat, and spend the next 20 minutes trying to remember how to install it. Back home, and he's had a feed and is sleeping in his Moses basket. I'm knackered. Jess is exhausted, and yelps every time she coughs on account of her tenderness. Isaac is excitable, and won't be calmed by *Shrek*, or even *Shrek 2*. But we're all fine, and that's the main thing – even if Jess is dreading her first post-birth poo.

But every silver lining must have a cloud: it cost me £7 to park at the hospital. Robbing gits.

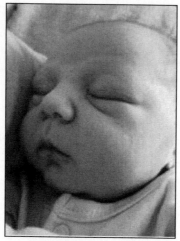

Noah William Wakeling
Born 22 April 2010

THE WEEK AFTER THE NIGHT BEFORE

Do you remember those Tamagotchi things that were a craze in the '90s? They were these little virtual pets, and you would press different buttons to wash it, feed it or put it to sleep. Well, having a baby is a lot like that,  although there's no 'off' button and you can't just stick a baby in your pocket and forget about it.

I've learned a lot during my first week of being a baby dad instead of a foetus dad, things I'd completely forgotten from last time around. And these things can be summarised in just a few headings.

Sleeping

"Hello, remember me? I'm Sleep. You may not recognise me, because we've not met in a week."

I'm sorry, that was poor at best, and not that funny. But take pity on me; I, like you (probably), have had little to no sleep this past week. On the plus side, I've discovered the joys of TV at two in the morning; and by 'joys', I mean mind-numbing boredom. Although I have to say: watching an empty-grinned, orange-skinned presenter with immaculate hair trying desperately to sell a vacuum cleaner to an audience of less than five is quite entertaining.

Depending on what kind of person you are, you may not mind being up every two hours in the night. I find that once I'm awake, after I've gotten past that stage where I want to cry, I'm not too bad. The biggest problem I have is that I'm incredibly short-sighted and my glasses are broken, meaning that I have to hold my face about six inches away from my son's rear end every time I change his nappy, which can prove dangerous.

This lack of sleep, combined with having a child, messes my brain up in a strange way. I find myself half-waking in the night, convinced that I'm lying on Noah, or that Jess is about to roll on top of him. This makes me start shrieking and clinging onto Jess' shoulders to stop her from turning over, which right royally cheeses her off; especially as, for some reason, I feel it necessary to yank the duvet off the bed each time. I don't recall any of this come the morning, but it's amusing to hear what I've done nonetheless; even if these tales are being recounted by my bleary-eyed wife through gritted teeth.

Fatherhood really helps you find your rhythm, though – you don't half pull some funky moves in an attempt to rock your baby back to sleep at 3am. I find the one that works best for me is to stand with both feet planted on the floor (always a good start) and do some kind of motion as if I'm roller blading, pushing with one foot then the other; not moving anywhere, of course, just swaying from side to side – similar to when I actually *do* roller blade.

Feeding

Don't try to feed your child yourself, if you both decide that breastfeeding is the way to go. Whilst you may possess a fine pair of nipples, you have no milk, and any attempt to get your child to latch on to one of your teats will only result in a very confused baby, a sore nipple and rejection by society.

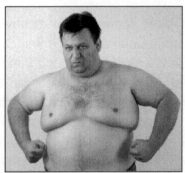

You may have man boobs, but they're still useless.

Jess is breastfeeding Noah, which means that I have little involvement in this side of things other than buying vats of nipple cream every week. To be honest, the whole thing looks pretty painful, which is another reason why I'm glad I'm not a woman, up there with having periods and lopsided breasts. The good news is, your mrs' boobs will now be even bigger as the milk kicks in, which is pretty awesome in itself. Not quite so awesome is the two-inch thick bra strap she needs to hold them up, but we'll just blast past that. Fortunately, she has not yet used her breast pump, and so I haven't been repulsed by this whirring piece of machinery that turns my wife into a cow, being milked for all she's worth.

Whether or not your mrs is breastfeeding, she may need to express milk from time to time. This is to help prevent such conditions as mastitis, which is caused by a blocked milk duct or bacterial infection, and is very painful.
Jess got this last time with Isaac, and was in a lot of discomfort; so I did a bit of research on the internet and found that some people  reckon putting a cabbage leaf in each bra cup can soothe the pain. And so we did, despite it being a bit odd, in the hope that it would help.

It didn't, and Jess' temperature rose to the point where she was beginning to get a bit delirious, eyes flitting about all over the place – very strange stuff, and scenes which would not look out of place in a Japanese horror movie. So, after a short while, we went to the hospital to get her checked out. I'll never forget the look on the doctor's face as he pulled down Jess' bra and two limp cabbage leaves flopped onto the floor with a pathetic slap, by this time smelling a bit funky. He looked at Jess, then at me, then back at Jess, a look of bizarre confusion etched across his face.

"Umm...we heard that it helps." I say, in a voice as feeble as the cabbage.

"...I don't think so." replies the doctor, and I am inclined to agree. He presses her boobs a bit, prescribes some antibiotics and paracetamol to bring down her temperature, and we leave, stooping to pick up two sad cabbage leaves on the way out.

Bottle feeding can be a great way to bond with your baby, and the chance for a quick cuddle. Next comes the burping, a seemingly endless routine of back patting and gentle bobbing up and down. Still, you can't help but feel a sense of achievement when your baby emits a wet belch after twenty minutes of patting.

Changing

Becoming a father provides you with a unique talent, but unfortunately one that won't give you superhero status. It is simply this: the ability to not freak out when you get baby poo on your finger. (You can see now why there would never be a superhero with this power, as it's completely pointless and won't save any lives.) You just wipe it off, job done, no panic. There does, however, come a point in your child's life where getting his or her poo on your finger *does* result in you dry retching over the carpet, and this unique talent goes out the window completely when getting adult poo on you, although hopefully this shouldn't happen too often, because that's what toilet paper is for.

Baby poo, in itself, is pretty gross, although fortunately it possesses quite a sweet smell, as opposed to adult poo which understandably smells rank. The first few turds your child does will bear all the consistency and colour of tar, clinging relentlessly to your baby's buttocks until you have to resort to pinching it off with a cotton wool ball. You may notice that the pooing is accompanied by a sharp squelch, and the odd eyelid flutter. Although the squelch slowly gives way to straining as your child grows older, the eyelid flutters never die.

I have found that the most important weapon in your arsenal when changing your child's nappy is not the warm water, or the cotton wool: but the scrunched-up ball of kitchen roll you keep close by at all times in case of little accidents. Now I have never fathered a girl, and so can only speak for boys – but when your baby boy decides to wee whilst you are in the middle of changing his nappy, you know about it.

It starts with a period of silence, which can only be described as sinister; this is because it comes unexpectedly whilst he is wriggling and crying on the changing mat. For the first couple of times, you wonder what is going on; but you soon learn that this is simply the calm before the storm. Don't be fooled into thinking he's calmed down, or is happy; he's just taking a few moments to aim.

Then, without warning, a little jet of pee arcs across the room like a watery yellow rainbow. I can only describe it as being akin to those spurts of liquid you see when doctors check that a syringe hasn't got any air in it; although, instead of a little spurt, it's a fountain that continues for far longer than it should, about the same duration as those wees you do after five pints of lager.

Quick as a flash, you grab the kitchen roll and attempt to stem the flow, turning up your nose as the paper almost instantly becomes soggy in your hand; and, inevitably, all his clothes are soaked and you have to completely change him.

There was one episode with my first child that I'm almost proud of, in a strange sort of way. I was changing him and had turned to the side to put his dirty nappy in a bag when I heard a strange gurgling sound, like someone blowing bubbles in a puddle of water. For a few seconds I looked around, completely bemused, until I turned back to Isaac to see him peeing on his own face with expert precision. Obviously, at the time, I diverted the stream straight away, as he was clearly getting a bit cheesed off; but in hindsight, it's quite a skill to have, and one that may get you through the first round of the various talent shows that litter the TV schedules, but probably no further – y'know, once the viewer complaints start pouring in.

By far and away the best part of changing Noah's nappy is picking him up afterwards. By the time you've struggled to stick the tabs on the nappy down because he refuses to straighten his legs, and fastened his vest and babygrow, Noah is pretty much screaming blue murder, throwing all kinds of shapes on the changing mat like a drunk old man at a wedding. I have no idea why he detests having his nappy changed so much, but I'm hoping that it doesn't carry through into later life. I'd hate to have a teenage son who cries whenever he changes his underwear; which, being a teenager, is probably once every few days.

But then I pick him up. Gradually, he stops vogueing and his cries die down as he burrows his face into my neck, and we have our post-change cuddle; one of my favourite times of the day. I give his cheek a few pecks, and – if he's hungry – he'll think that I'm trying to feed him and kiss me back by repeatedly yet softly butting my face with his mouth; and suddenly it doesn't matter that a few minutes previously you had your best shirt soaked by a jet of baby pee.

A word of warning, to conclude this section: those little fasteners on baby clothing ('poppers', as they're sometimes called) are impossible to do up if your baby is crying. Somehow, the two are related, and you'll find yourself in such a rush to get him or her dressed that instead of thinking about it logically, locating both sides of the popper and pressing them together, you'll just randomly pinch pieces of material, hoping that you somehow strike lucky; and, if it doesn't work, you just pinch harder.

Washing

As with all babies, when Noah was first born he wasn't the cleanest of creatures. Half of his scalp was smeared with blood, and the rest of him was a bit slimy, even after a vigorous buffing by two midwives armed with towels. This combination of blood and goo was the reason for my first skin to skin contact with my newborn son being a tentative 'cootchy-coo' on his forehead with one stretched index finger from an arms length away.

A few wipes later with a couple of those brilliant cotton wool ball inventions, and the majority of goo was gone, save for a few persistent bits which matted parts of his soft hair.

I'll be honest – those remnants of goo lasted for a good day or so, until we gave Noah his first bath. Safe to say, he was not a fan. That boy screamed the house down, and when you think about it, you can understand why. Here is a baby who has been surrounded by fluid for a good nine months, cramped and sweaty. Finally, after being pushed out – which, for a baby, must be the most bemusing of happenings – he's free, able to wriggle his arms and legs about, whilst screaming and crying. He's also able to poop without having to worry too much, because he isn't in the womb any more, and crimping out a poo in the womb is like passing wind whilst trapped in a kitchen cupboard; there's no way out.

So, then, it's understandable that – upon being immersed in water once again – Noah began to freak out. I guess it's either that that made him cry, or the fact that we were looking at his weird crispy belly button thing, and he was feeling self-conscious.

Better get him out of the bath before things get violent.

Fortunately, this did not repeat itself the next time we bathed him, and now when we dunk Noah in the bath he floats there quite happily, supported by one of our arms of course. This silence is good for us, although it is a bit annoying that he can't shampoo his own hair yet.

Visitors

Practically from the moment we stepped through the front door of our house for the first time with Noah, people were queuing up, clutching cards in one hand and presents in the other. One by one they'd file in and take a look at the new arrival; some would try to think of a novel remark, other than the clichéd "Oh, isn't he *beautiful*?" but fail, instead standing there with hands clasped awkwardly in front of them as they smack their lips whilst thinking of something to say. You'll get the obvious questions time and time again: "How is he sleeping?" "Does he cry a lot?" "Are you feeding him yourself?" – word of warning: that last question is for the mother only.

I have found that some relatives and friends are, for whatever reason, not fully satisfied at seeing Noah when he is asleep, instead moaning politely about wanting to see him with his eyes open. Why it makes such a difference is beyond me, like seeing him when he's awake allows them to give a better judgement on whether they like him or not, but as with many visitors you sit and grin inanely whilst you show off your new arrival. Sometimes, the sheer volume of visitors will begin to bug you, as well as the incessant text messages and phone calls asking what time is best to come over; but it is a chance to proudly display the fruit of your loins, as well as bag a bunch of presents in the process.

How would you sum up the first week? Well, I miss being able to go to bed at night and waking up in the morning, uninterrupted. But the truth is, the next day, you don't really remember being awake in the night - probably because you rock your son or daughter to sleep in a bit of a daze, with your hair all a mess and dried dribble on your cheek.

I miss chilling out in the evenings, without having to run up the stairs once every five minutes to soothe a child whose cries I've just heard over the static of the baby monitor. But the truth is, cuddling my little boy as he falls asleep in my arms is miles better than any episode of *Scrubs* that I've seen countless times before.

I miss being able to simply stick my shoes on and leave the house; I now – with Jess' help – have to assemble a cumbersome pram, force a car seat into the back of my Honda, bow under the weight of three bags of baby toys and change a nappy in the middle of Boots as old women turn up their nose and look disapprovingly at me. But the truth is, I want to show the world our little guy, and in turn show my baby the big bad world that he will grow up in, and reassure myself that I can protect him from any danger that will ever come his way.

And so, the first week has had its ups and downs, its highlights and lowlights. We've had sick, poo, and tears; cuddles, kisses and a bunch of presents. And I wouldn't change a minute of it for the world.

Anyway, I have to go: Noah is crying again and it's my turn to work out whether he needs feeding, burping or changing, and then press the correct button on my tiny screaming Tamagotchi.

FATHERHOOD AND YOUR JOB

Fortunately, we've come a long way from the middle of last century. In the 1940s and 50s, a man would be told that he was going to be a father; in response, he would twiddle his moustache and tell his wife to come back in nine months. In the 1960s, men were too busy back-combing their hair and getting high to even realise that they'd gotten some poor girl pregnant in a festival tent. When the 1970s came, fathers were becoming more interested, but barred from entering the delivery suite by a  broad-shouldered ageing midwife who had a hint of moustache and, disturbingly, beard.

Things are different now, and the majority of dads want to be involved. Fortunately, the UK Government has recognised this and laid down laws that mean we get time off work and a bit of pay to help look after our baby when it makes its grand entrance into the world.

The first thing to do when looking into what kind of paternity leave and pay you get is start digging around in your company's policies and procedures. A lot of businesses will have their own arrangements, many of which are better than the Government's Statutory Paternity Leave and Pay. If there is no policy, or it's not very good, you can go for the Government scheme.

Paternity Leave

Legally, you are responsible for telling your employer that your partner is pregnant, although they may well have  guessed on account of your thousand-yard stare and shaking hands. You need to let them know when your baby is due, or – if you are adopting – when you expect the child to be placed with you. You're also required to give them the correct amount of notice, which is at least 15 weeks before the beginning of the week when the baby is due – before week 25, essentially. This is best done via an 'SC3' form, which is available for download online. Please bear in mind that if you're reading this book a few hundred years from now, the aliens (or rabbits) that have taken over the world may have different procedures in place, and they may involve probing.

The good news is you don't need to give your employer any medical evidence of the pregnancy, which means that you can avoid placing a small pot of pregnancy wee on his desk, or – better still – dipping the positive test in his cup of tea.

In the UK, you are entitled to one or two weeks of paternity leave, but they must be taken consecutively and as a block – you can't have the odd day here and there to make up the two weeks. Just let your employer know the date you want your paternity leave to start when you tell them that your mrs is expecting. Leave can begin on any day of the week on or following the child's birth, but you must have taken it within eight weeks of your baby being born, or eight weeks from the expected date of birth if your baby is born early.

Antenatal Classes

The dad does not have a legal right to time off so he can go with his partner to antenatal appointments, but unless they're made out of stone (or you work for the Nazis) your manager will normally give you a few hours or a day off as long as you make up the time afterwards. They're not daft; they know full well that if you want to go to the scans with your partner and they don't give you time off, you'll magically develop a 24-hour bug on the morning of each appointment day. You might also throw in graphic tales of explosive diarrhoea when you call in sick, just to give it some kind of weight.

Statutory Paternity Pay

This is what you're really interested in, isn't it? Again: check your company's policies, as they may quite happily give you time off with full pay as you wrestle with a newborn baby (figuratively, of course). To be eligible for Statutory Paternity Pay from the Government, which is paid by your employer, you need to tick a few boxes:

- You must be the biological father of the child, or the mother's husband or partner, responsible for the child's upbringing;
- You must have been working for your employer continuously for at least 26 weeks by the time the 15th week before your baby is due comes around;
- You must carry on working uninterrupted for the same employer up until the baby is born;
- You must be earning at least £97 a week (before tax) on average.

If you can say 'Yes' to all these things, then you need to stop talking out loud to yourself. People will think you're weird. But you will be entitled to SPP.

So what actually goes into your pocket for you to spend on nappies, wipes, more nappies and your baby's first football kit? At the time of writing, if you get over the £97/week threshold, you'll receive £124.88 per week for the one or two weeks that you take off. If you earn less than £97/week, you'll get 90 percent of your average weekly earnings. It'll come in through your normal wages as per usual, and as such is subject to tax and National Insurance deductions (robbing gits). If you have more than one job, you might be able to get Statutory Paternity Pay from each employer, which would be pretty good.

If you reckon your employer is wrong

If your bosses are refusing to pay you Statutory Paternity Pay and you reckon they're talking bobbins, then your first port of call is to speak to them to find out exactly why they've come to this tight-fisted conclusion.

"What can I say? It's 'cos I don't like you."

If their reasons are rubbish, then the next step is to go through your company's grievance procedure – if they have one – and make a formal complaint. If that doesn't work out, you can get in touch with HM Revenue and Customs on 0845 3021479 for advice. There's tonnes of resources available on the internet as well, so do your homework to make sure that you're eligible and have a case.

Your Entitlements

Your annual paid holiday allowance will not be affected by going on paternity leave, although you can't take annual leave during that time. You can, however, if you're really nifty, take some annual leave straight after your paternity leave if you want a bit more time off.

If your employer contributes to a pension scheme, then this continues unaffected whilst you're on paternity leave. If you normally make contributions, just carry on with it. You'll reap the rewards when you're old and grey, and wetting yourself.

Unless you've been made redundant in the time you're on paternity leave, which would really suck, you have the right to return to your job under the same terms and conditions of employment you had before. You are also entitled to benefit from any pay rises or bonuses that are handed out whilst you're off.

If you want more time off after paternity leave to look after your child, you may be entitled to parental leave. This will not impact your ability to return to the same job. Alternatively, you can look into flexible working hours or working from home.

Checklist

Have you...

- ☐ Looked into your company's internal paternity policies?
- ☐ Told your employer that your mrs is pregnant and when the baby is due?
- ☐ Told them this in good time (prior to the 15th week before the estimated due date)?
- ☐ Told them if you want one or two weeks of leave and when you want the leave to start?
- ☐ Hugged a tree today?

Sources Used
Directgov
http://www.direct.gov.uk

FATHERHOOD AND YOUR WALLET

In February of 2010, a major UK newspaper reported on its website that the cost of raising a child in this day and age is around the £200,000 mark. Now, I don't know exactly how that is broken down, but it doesn't take a genius to work out that it's a heck of a lot of cash.

You have probably already noticed the costs mounting up: the pram, the cot, decorating the room – that, in itself, can cost the best part of a grand, depending on how far you go. But it's the things you don't really notice that add up over time and make the biggest dent in your bank  balance: the tonnes of nappies that you'll buy, for example – and they aren't cheap. Clothes, too, can be pretty expensive, as the savvy retailers realise that buying clothes for your child is somewhat unavoidable, unless you attempt to manufacture your own clothes out of tin foil and pillowcases.

The good news is that there are laws and legislations in place to help you out financially at this time. I won't go into loads of detail, firstly because it'll bore you to tears, and secondly because I don't want to. Do some work yourself, you lazy git!

Government Help

The criteria for qualification change all the time, but your mrs will probably be eligible for Maternity Allowance, if she can't get Statutory Maternity Pay from her employer.

Getting Maternity Allowance all depends on whether she meets certain criteria:

- Employed, but not eligible for Statutory Maternity Pay;
- Registered as self-employed and paying Class 2 National Insurance Contributions, or holds a Small Earnings Exception Certificate;
- She has very recently been employed or self-employed.
- She's been employed and/or self-employed for at least 26 weeks in her 'test period', which is 66 weeks up to and including the week before the week your baby is due);
- She earned £30 a week averaged over any 13 weeks in her test period.

All this information, along with details of her earnings, goes into working out if she is eligible for Maternity Allowance, and how much she'll get. At the moment, it's paid at a standard weekly rate of £124.88, or 90 percent of her average weekly earnings before tax, whichever is the smaller, because that's how the Government works. Meanies. It's paid for 39 weeks every fortnight or four weeks, and the earliest she can claim it is from the 11th week before your baby's due date. The latest is from the day following your baby's birth. You can appeal if you're refused Maternity Allowance.

You then have other financial help at hand such as Child Benefit. If you have one kid, you pocket around £20.30 a week, and £13.40 per week for every child after that.

Tax Credits can also be claimed, based on your circumstances and income. Because of this it's hard to pin down exactly how much a week you'll get – it's best if you get onto the internet and do some digging. The Government do give you an example online, though:

Mr and Mrs Khan both work full-time. Between them, they earn about £25,000 a year. They have three children. They get about £92 a week in tax credits.

Nice little earner, although I think making a living out of churning out kids would take its toll pretty quickly.

Your mrs can also claim a 'Health in Pregnancy' grant, to help you out when buying baby stuff. She can claim this from Week 25 of her pregnancy after filling out a form from her midwife: the current amount is £190. This doesn't double if you're expecting twins, but nice try all the same.

Other Ways of Saving Cash

Whilst these allowances and grants undoubtedly help you out, there are also a number of ways in which you can save money on various items, which will make your bank balance look healthier. A lot of people will dispute that you spend £200,000 raising a kid, and rightly so; a lot of items tagged as 'essential' aren't really essential at all. Who needs a cot when you can buy a baby hammock? (Just kidding. Although a baby hammock is an awesome idea.)

I just Googled 'baby hammocks'. They exist.

Make a Gift List

Word of warning: people are going to buy the new baby clothes, clothes, and more clothes; and, most of the time, they'll be pretty horrible. Some may try something slightly different and buy clothes for a few months old, but not think about what the weather will probably be like at that time. So, you'll get a sweet 3 month-old t-shirt and shorts outfit for a baby that will be subjected to sleet and hail when it reaches that age.

The best way to get around this – and get a wider range of stuff you need for your baby – is to create a gift list and distribute it to family and friends before the birth, much like a wedding gift list. People can then choose an item and buy it for you, meaning that you end up with a lot of different things that you actually need and want, instead of wading waist-high through a sea of baby vests adorned with whimsical sayings.

Hand-Me-Downs

There's no shame in accepting hand-me-downs from friends and family once your baby arrives; indeed, it might be impossible to avoid it, as people who you never normally talk to jump at the chance to get rid of the old baby clothes and toys that have been clogging up their loft for years.

It's not really a problem, unless you're *really* proud; your baby isn't going to give a monkey's if it's dressed in second-hand stuff. You might even hit the jackpot, with people donating things like cots and prams, which can cost a fortune to buy. As long as they're safe to use, you're golden.

Get Yer Boobs Out

Not you, so put your shirt down. I'm talking about breastfeeding.

Bottle vs Breast is a decision that all parents need to take at some point during pregnancy – you can see all the pros and cons listed in another chapter. It is safe to say, though, that feeding your baby with milk produced for free is a heck of a lot cheaper than buying powdered formula milk every few weeks, as well as the sterilising equipment and bottles that go with it. Yes, it might result in a cracked nipple or two, but at least your bank balance will be a bit healthier. Unfortunately, some mothers simply cannot breastfeed, or may feel pressured into breastfeeding. Remember: it's your choice, no-one else's.

If your mrs can put up with the ridiculous social stigma that is attached with breastfeeding in public, or the odd inquisitive teenager who peeks out of the corner of his eye as he meanders past, then this is a sure-fire way to save a heap of cash.

Buy Larger Clothes

Babies grow fast. I'm not talking Jack and the Beanstalk fast, but it won't be long before you start noticing that he or she is a bit bigger and heavier than they were when first born. Because of this, some baby clothes will last for a few weeks tops before they become too small and get stored in the garage to become progressively mouldier over time.

Your best bet is to buy baby clothes that are slightly larger than you need, so the baby can grow into them and you get your money's worth. Obviously, there's a line: if you stick your baby in a pair of adult-size Levis and a long-sleeved shirt/tie combo from Next it's going to look pretty ridiculous. Use your noggin, for crying out loud.

Stick to Essential Items

People have been having babies for thousands of years, long before the days when cots, prams, baby carriers and musical mobiles were around; and they were raised fine, apart from being perhaps a bit grubby, especially if they were peasants.

A lot of baby items that are advertised as being 'must have' are not 'must have' at all. In reality, you only need a few basic things in order to raise your child, and just because you don't have the latest all-singing, all-dancing automatically rocking baby basket doesn't make you any less of a parent.

Obviously, there are some items that are unavoidable, such as clothing and bedding – but if you look around, you can pick up a bargain with little to no difficulty. Make a list of what you reckon the fundamental items are before the baby arrives and see how you get on.

Your baby doesn't have to cost the earth. The things it really needs aren't expensive at all: to be brought up in a family and home that is comfortable, loving and protective. And also, one that has a Playstation.

Sources Used
The Guardian, "How much does it cost to raise a child?", 23
February 2010
http://www.guardian.co.uk/money/2010/feb/23/child-cost-inflation

Directgov
http://www.direct.gov.uk

FATHERHOOD AND YOUR RELATIONSHIP

Bad news: having your month-old in a baby carrier as you boogie the night away on the dance floor is not a good look, and will also probably get you into trouble with Social Services.

The fact of the matter is this: becoming a father changes *everything*. Those who say it hasn't changed their lives one bit probably didn't have a life to begin with, and you have my permission to deliver a stinging backhand to the face. It will change your social life, your bank balance - even your health, if you really become sleep deprived. But one thing it will probably change the most is your relationship with the mrs.

This is not necessarily a bad thing: change doesn't have to be terrible, and I'm certainly not saying that after the birth of your child you'll be on a fast train to Splitsville: however, there have been a number of studies undertaken on the relationship quality and overall happiness of couples who have recently had a baby; and they demonstrate that immediately following the birth of your kid, many couples note a decline in their relationship.

Here's some figures to back this up. There was some research carried out back in the early part of this century by University of Washington student Alyson Shapiro and John Gottman, a well-respected marital researcher who has a PhD to his name. The results were published in a report entitled (deep breath) "The baby and the marriage: identifying factors that buffer against decline in marital satisfaction after the first baby arrives", published in the *Journal of Family Psychology*.

These two bright minds selected 82 couples who were in their first year of marriage and observed them for around four to six years. During that time, 43 of the couples  became parents, and 39 remained childless. Interviews and tests were held with both mum and dad after the baby, and the results found that about a year after the baby was born both mothers and fathers noted a decline in their relationship satisfaction; 67% of mothers reported declines, whilst 56% of fathers noted the same dissatisfaction.

It seems, from the results, that immediately following birth relationship happiness declines a bit, but is often masked by the fact that both parents are chuffed to have a baby. Then, after about a year, the novelty of having a kid has worn off, and any cracks begin to show.

Some other boffins named Jay Belsky and John Kelly carried out some similar research back in 1994, and found that arguments between new parents arose in five main areas:

Household chores. Yeah, you can't expect her to make your sandwiches *all* the time now. And you may be called upon to iron whilst your mrs is temporarily incapacitated by feeding your baby.

Money. Or lack of it. Babies are expensive things, and your beer fund may be severely dented, instead being used to buy nappies or nipple pads.

Work. Many couple just assume that the father will carry on working whilst the mum stays at home to bring up the child. Fact is, there are tonnes of Stay At Home Dads (or SAHDs) out there who opt to do the raising whilst the mum dons her pencil skirt and heads back into the world of work.

Relationship. Now there's an addition to your family, you might not have as much time for each other – plus, after a long day of feeding, burping and continuous rocking, you're both going to be too tired to…well, y'know. This can cause issues, especially as you threaten to trawl the street corners and risk a savage STD just to get some action.

Social Life. There's no doubt about it, having a kid puts some serious strain on your social life, and you will probably find that you aren't able to go out as much as you used to, either individually or together. But think of the money you'll save by simply staying in and watching *Coronation Street*!

So, pretty depressing stuff; but don't pick up the phone to Relate just yet. Just because that's what the numbers say, doesn't mean that it'll happen to you.

One important thing the research did pick up on was that couples who resolved any arguments in a mutually satisfying way (i.e. you don't start slamming around and demanding you get to go to the pub) are far more likely to work together to overcome problems, and as a result have a happy and healthy relationship. Plus, there's nothing wrong with having someone over to babysit every now and again whilst you go out and let your hair down (unless you're bald, in which case substitute 'let your hair down' with 'wax your dome').

Warning: You may now dance like your father.

These studies also showed that couples who had a happy relationship before having a baby were much more likely to continue to be satisfied after the little sprog entered their lives, which is why having a kid to save a marriage rarely works. The main thing is to stick together, and recognise that you're both under a lot of stress and going through a massive life change. If you talk to each other, respect your mrs' views and support one another whenever possible – as well as, now and again, taking time out to hang with each other, go out for a meal, that kind of thing – there's no reason why anything should change for worse at all.

And get your washing up gloves on. They make you look dashing.

FATHERHOOD AND YOUR RIGHTS

With the best will in the world, sometimes things just don't work out. Whether it's the strain of having a baby, or cracks opening up for a completely different reason, some dads find themselves separated from the mother of their children.

If this is your situation, you can be forgiven for thinking that this is the end of the line, that your child will be put into the mother's care, and that you'll rarely see them. However, this is certainly not the case, and there is a wealth of resource out there for single fathers looking to find out what rights they have. This chapter is just a brief overview, and if you would like to find out more there are a number of websites out there that can help – just check out the 'Useful Links' page near the back of this book.

Parental Responsibility

The first thing to do is ascertain whether or not you have parental responsibility for your child. This is defined by law as 'all the rights, duties, powers, responsibility and authority which by law a parent of a child has in relation to the child and his property.'

What that basically means is that if you have any say in bringing up the child, arranging the child's education, having contact with it, that kind of thing, then you have parental responsibility. Similarly, if you were married at the time of birth, or if your name is on the child's birth certificate (assuming the child was born after 1 December 2003) then you automatically have parental responsibility. If you don't legally have parental responsibility, you can apply for it in the courts.

Financial Help

You may be required to pay towards the upbringing of your child through what are known as maintenance payments. In the vast majority of cases, the amount of payment can be settled away from the courts in a civil conversation between mother and father, where you can also decide how often it is paid, that kind of thing.

The parent who has care of the child (because the child doesn't always get put under the care of its mother) can, if a private agreement can't be reached, apply to the Child Support Agency for maintenance money. He or she can also apply for a lump sum payment or for the transfer of property, these things being decided in the Family Proceedings Court or the County Court.

Various things are taken into account by the Court when working out an Order, including:

- The income of each party;
- The financial needs of the child;
- The financial needs of each parent;
- Any physical or mental disability of the child.

The best advice that I can give is to speak to your solicitors for further information and guidance.

Visiting Your Child

Each parent has the right to see their child after a split has occurred; it's the law (said Judge Dredd-style). The only way in which a parent would be prohibited from seeing their child would be if there was a legitimate concern that the parent would try to take the child away and run off with it. If this is the case then the Court may pass an order stating that the parent can only visit their child if someone else is present to supervise them, or in a public location.

Having Your Child Visit You

Again, in many cases, the mum and dad can come to an amicable agreement about visiting rights, and whether your child can come to visit you or even stay with you for a few days.

If things are a bit strained, you can go to the courts to apply for a Contact Order, which will require the carer of the child to let him or her come to visit. As with all decisions made in the courts, the welfare of the child is the biggest factor determining the outcome. They'll look at such things like:

- Whether the child wants to visit you;
- The child's physical, emotional and educational needs;
- Any harm which the child has suffered or is at risk of suffering.

Applying for Custody

Since 1989 in the UK, custody orders have been replaced with Residence Orders, which regulate where a child is to live. This will normally be decided in the Magistrates Court, the County Court, or – in difficult cases – the High Court.

It's an unfortunate truth for fathers that, in most cases, the mother gets sole custody of the child. However, if it can be proven that the mother is not fit to take care of the child, then the father will be the sole carer.

Another option is a Joint Residence Order, something which is very popular in the US. This will only be granted if the court is persuaded that both parents are happy with the agreement, can make it work and it is in the best interests of the child.

This can be a difficult and troubling time. With all these things, if decisions can be kept out of the courts it will save a lot of grief and time for everyone involved, as well as limiting any unhappiness for the child. Over time, things will get better – and if you are unsure of your rights, then talk to your solicitor. If you are feeling depressed, then make sure you talk to a professional as well as getting as much support as you can from family and friends.

Sources Used

Information taken primarily from www.onlydads.org, one of the UK's top resources for single fathers.

Law and Parents: Single Parents' Rights
http://www.lawandparents.co.uk/single-parents-rights.html

Directgov: Parental rights and responsibilities
http://www.direct.gov.uk/en/Parents/parentsrights/DG_400295
4

FATHERHOOD AND YOU

Let's face it; you're a man. And, as a man, you tend not to cry an awful lot. In fact, the last time you got a lump in your throat was when England won the Rugby World Cup in 2003, or that night your mrs finally wore the sexy underwear you'd bought for her two years earlier. It was almost definitely not when that old woman chucked the necklace in the sea at the end of *Titanic*, no sir. That was just something in my eye, honest.

Stop looking at me like that, *Titanic* lady. I'll never admit it.

The thing is, though, pregnancy and the resulting birth of your child makes you a lot more sensitive than you were before. You'll find yourself getting angrier than you would have done previously when you read a news story about child abuse, and you won't feel quite so bloodthirsty when an alligator chomps down on a baby bird in one of those TV wildlife programmes.

You'll also become much more protective, and the mere thought of someone or something making your child upset or hurting even a hair on their head makes your blood boil. If your kid gets picked on in school, you'll want to head down there straight away and deliver a flying knee kick to the bullies' faces, even if they are about eight years old. But this is normal: the feelings, that is; not the kung-fu moves on prepubescent children. That's illegal, apparently.

Pregnancy, as well as being an exciting time, can also be very worrying, as you fret about the change to your life that your child will bring. And there will be changes, make no mistake.

It's just as important during pregnancy for you to take time out for yourself, as well as looking after your mrs. Even the tightest of couples need their own space sometimes, so don't feel bad about taking a few hours to go down to the pub, watch a football match, or play a round of golf. Of course, there are exceptions, and quality 'me' time should be in moderation. A two-week  holiday for one to Mauritius may cause a bit of tension, as would spending your partner's due date in the local casino, blowing your life savings on Blackjack.

Bottom line is, pregnancy and the birth of your child changes everything. It changes you, it changes your partner, and it changes your relationship. But change doesn't have to be a bad thing; you'll have a tiny boy or girl who looks up to you, who will learn life skills from you, and will know that you will protect them, no matter what. And they'll love you for it; and, at the end of the day, nothing matters more than that.

Well, *almost* noth- no, wait: **nothing.** Focus, Ben!

DECISIONS: BREAST OR BOTTLE?

Breast! Oh, wait, you're talking about feeding.

The decision of whether or not your mrs breastfeeds your baby is one faced by every new parents. All the posters you see tacked up on hospital walls tell you that 'breast is best', which can put a mother who either doesn't want to breastfeed – or *can't* – under a lot of pressure, making them feel as if they're somehow less of a mum.

A study by the Office for National Statistics in the UK, however, threw up some interesting results. They found that in 2005, only 35 percent of babies were being exclusively breastfed at one week old, 21 percent at six weeks, and 7 percent at four months; and whilst this is up by 7 percent on the previous study in 2000, it is perhaps surprising – and reassuring – for those who are planning on purely bottle feeding to know that they are not alone.

The thing is, these guys have got a point when they say that 'breast is best'. The advantages of breastfeeding are well documented, much like the inside of Britney Spears' thighs, but we'll run through them again here – as well as the disadvantages, because there are some of those too. And, on the other side of the coin, there are pros and cons to bottle feeding as well. I'm not here to make your choice for you; I'm here simply to give you the facts and try to throw in a spattering of humour so it doesn't feel like you're back at school.

Let's talk a little bit about breasts. Well, to be exact – breastfeeding. Whether you want to believe it or not, those jubblies hanging from the front of your mrs are there for more than just your goggle-eyed enjoyment. Paediatricians, doctors, midwifes – you name it, the vast majority of medical experts will insist that these lady lumps be used for their rightful purpose: feeding your child. It's the ideal food for your baby: it has the nutrients that he or she needs, getting the 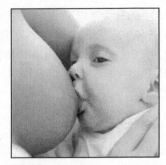 blend of vitamins, minerals, digestive enzymes, fat, sugars and protein just right, not unlike a Mars Bar – although the fat/sugar, vitamin/mineral ratios might be a bit out. As well as this, breast milk reduces the risk of a number of infant illnesses, such as pneumonia, bronchitis, meningitis, and diarrhoea.

The benefits don't just stop at baby. For your partner, whose mind will already be on burning off the pregnancy flab, breastfeeding burns around 500 calories a day. To put this into perspective, that's like running non-stop for 4-5 miles. It seems that women have the perfect exercise regime, but like selfish oiks they're keeping it to their own gender.

As well as the calorie-burning thing, breastfeeding helps your partner's uterus contract back to its normal size more quickly, something which can be pretty painful; again, to put this into perspective, her uterus is going from the size of a small beach ball to an organ about three inches long in a relatively short space of time.

Another benefit can be found in the realms of finance. Unless you frequent some rather seedy establishments, or pay thousands of pounds to get perky puppies, boobs are free, and so is the milk. And, because the milky goodness is attached to your mrs at all times, your baby can be fed wherever and whenever the need arises – however, be wary of some who frown upon public breastfeeding; wrongly, in my opinion.

There are also emotional benefits for mother and baby. Mums who breastfeed often find themselves more attached to their children – and, before you say it, not physically, although you are correct: one gold star. The hormones that she produces whilst breastfeeding can promote motherly feelings, and cement the bond between mum and baby. Unfortunately, that leaves you somewhat out of the loop, as your child invades your territory and sets up camp rent-free.

This brings us on to the disadvantages of breastfeeding. You run the risk of feeling a bit left out if you're not involved in this side of things, and so it's important to discuss which option you're going to go with before the baby's born. However, you can get involved just after the feed: you can burp your kid, which may not seem like a plus when he or she pukes all over your best shirt. Alternatively, if your mrs is going to be away or unable to feed for a while, she can use one of those hideous breast pump devices to express a few ounces of milk, and then you can do the feeding for once.

Breast pumps are handy, but you can't help but think of this.

The mum needs to keep an eye on what she's putting in her body when breastfeeding. Caffeine can cause problems, and some foods might give your baby gas or allergic reactions. And, of course: no alcohol, drugs or smoking when feeding. Despite conjuring up a frankly revolting image in your mind of your mrs - boob out, spliff between lips, clutching a bottle of Jack Daniels and popping Nurofen whilst (for some reason) dancing as if she's in a sweaty rave – it can cause mega complications in your child.

It is also possible that, when breastfeeding, your mrs will suffer from cracked nipples, mastitis, engorgement – all of which are very painful. It is, however, a myth that your mrs' boobs will get all saggy like spaniel's ears if she breastfeeds: unfortunately, this is a result of pregnancy as a whole, not just breastfeeding. Aww, nuts.

So what about bottle feeding? Whilst breastfeeding does give your baby nutrients and antibodies that aren't yet found in formula milk, technology has advanced enough to be pretty darn close. Bottom line is: you're not going to be putting your baby's health at risk by bottle feeding, so you don't need to worry. With bottle feeding, you – the dad – get to feed your baby, thus helping you bond with him or her; and this can be shared with other family members who want a slice of the fun. Your mrs will thank you as well, for giving her more time to get on with her chores, like doing her make-up, jabbering with her mates, or making you a sandwich. And, in her free time, she can drink coffee and tea until it's coming out of her ears, as well as the odd glass of wine. She can also take prescription drugs as and when required; illegal drugs, unsurprisingly, are still off-limits.

Back away from the spliff!

Bottle feeding also has the advantage over breastfeeding in that you know exactly how much food your baby is getting, and because of this babies generally sleep longer between feeds.

This, though, gives you more time to go out to the shops and buy the formula powder in the first place, and let me warn you: it ain't cheap. Throughout the first few months of your child's life you'll easily rack up a few hundred quid buying the formula, as well as spending time preparing it in the middle of the night whilst you're all bleary-eyed and your balance is rubbish. As well as the formula, you'll need to buy bottles and teats, and the sterilising equipment needed to zap those nasty bugs.

So there you go: those are the cold, hard facts. It is important to stress that there is no right or wrong decision to make. Each couple will choose a path that works best for them, and you guys will be no different. And don't worry: soon, those boobs will be yours again.

BREAST vs BOTTLE: THE SHOWDOWN

BREAST

Advantages
- Free
- Nutritious
- Protects baby against many illnesses
- Possibly protects mum against ovarian cancer, breast cancer and osteoporosis
- Helps mum lose weight
- Quickens contractions of the uterus
- May improve child's mental development
- Close bond between mum and baby
- No equipment required, just a boob or two

Disadvantages
- Reduced caffeine intake required
- No alcohol or drugs
- Some food might cause complications with baby
- Breastfeeding in public might cause issues
- Have to breastfeed quite often
- Little control over how much milk your baby gets

BOTTLE

Advantages

- Babies sleep for longer between feeds
- You can regulate how much he/she has
- Similar nutrient level as breast milk
- Dads can get in on the feeding gig
- Formula milk has added Vitamin K

Disadvantages

- Increased chance of infection or illness
- Risk of mistakes when preparing milk
- Equipment and sterilisation required
- Expensive

Sources Used
Unicef: The Baby Friendly Initiative - UK Breastfeeding Rates
http://www.babyfriendly.org.uk/page.asp?page=21

NHS: Advantages/Disadvantages of Breast and Bottle Feeding
http://www.nhs.uk/Conditions/Bottle-feeding/Pages/Advantages.aspx
http://www.nhs.uk/Conditions/Bottle-feeding/Pages/Disadvantages.aspx

Bupa: Breastfeeding
http://hcd2.bupa.co.uk/fact_sheets/html/breastfeeding.html

DECISIONS: HOME OR HOSPITAL

Have you ever thought 'Well, yeah, I'd love to be present at the birth of my child, but I'd also like to watch *Die Hard* at the same time on my 50-inch plasma'? It's a fantasy shared by many men, I'm sure. Similarly, your mrs might feel the same way (only substituting *Sex and the City* instead of *Die Hard*) in which case, a  home birth might be a pretty good option for you. It's worth saying at this point that home birth isn't a viable option for every mum; some are 'high risk', due to age or health problems, and will be required to give birth in a hospital. If you're unsure, it's always best to talk it through with your midwife.

It's protocol for first-time parents to have their baby in a hospital, just to be on the safe side; but this isn't compulsory, and a home birth is an option for all expectant parents. There are a number of advantages and disadvantages to home and hospital birth, which are laid out before you in this book for your perusal.

HOME BIRTH

Advantages

Perhaps the main advantage of a home birth is the fact that you and your partner are in familiar surroundings. This will help her to relax more, and allow her to carry on with household chores and make you plenty of cups of tea.

JOKE.

She can also watch TV if she likes, and your baby can crown away to the sound of the *EastEnders* theme tune in the background, before both mum and baby chill out in a familiar bed.

The fact that she is more relaxed means that her body will produce endorphins, the feel-good hormones that will calm her down and relax her muscles. Studies have shown that this leads to a less painful labour, which in turn means less screaming.

Studies have also shown that mothers who have a home birth are less likely to need to go through

Caesareans or assisted delivery. The midwife will also bring pain relief with her, such as gas and air or pethidine, which you'll need to obtain from your GP before labour day as midwives can only administer controlled medicine, not prescribe it.

The birth is attended by one or two midwives that you've gotten to know throughout the pregnancy, and have built up some kind of rapport with. These midwives will stay with you both throughout labour and birth, providing one-to-one care, as well as making regular visits for a few days afterwards to check everything's OK.

Although a very rare occurrence in hospital, having your baby at home pretty much eliminates the risk of it being nicked by a crazy person.

Disadvantages

Whilst pain relief is provided by the midwife, she cannot administer an epidural – so if things get too painful you and your mrs will need to head into hospital. You need to have a look at how close your nearest hospital is, as a long journey could cause problems if your partner is having complications.

Even though you have the latest and sharpest set of kitchen knives, there's no way that a Caesarean can be performed in the home. If anything, it'd freak out passers-by who happened to look in the window at the wrong moment. You also can't have a ventouse or forceps delivery at home, and so if these are required it means a trip down to hospital.

Whilst your mrs will be in her own bed after birth, it does mean that she's probably going to ruin your finest Egyptian cotton sheets. Plus, you won't have any staff there to change sheets or provide meals for you – that role, my friend, is down to you.

HOSPITAL BIRTH

Advantages

Being in a hospital brings with it peace of mind that your mrs will receive the best care possible by a team of experts, and that they'll be on hand at a moment's notice.

Also, if things are getting too much, the mum can receive an epidural to help kill the pain and relax her. Unfortunately, you're not allowed one, although I do think it'd make you look funny as you tried to keep your balance once your legs started going numb. You'd look like Bambi learning how to walk.

Not Bambi's mum. She got shot.

If things get messy and bedsheets get ruined, you don't need to worry about it. Someone will come along, clean all that up and give your partner some nice clean sheets to subsequently bleed on again.

Another advantage is that there are no long journeys to hospital or traffic jams to worry about if things start going wrong; they'll just wheel her down the corridor to the operating room and get to work.

A lot of the post-natal tests on your baby, such as a hearing check, paediatric check, etc. can be done whilst in hospital, meaning you don't all have to keep trekking to your local doctors or make appointments for them to come to you.

Disadvantages

You'll be in a place which is probably unfamiliar, which can be unsettling for both you and mum, causing her to become more tense and therefore possibly resulting in a more painful labour.

Although your mrs will get constant care whilst in the throes of childbirth, you probably won't get one-to-one assistance whilst contracting in the ward, as there will be a small team of midwives looking after a big group of dilating women.

Hospitals are susceptible to outbreaks of disease and infection, which could put mum and baby at risk if it spreads enough. Also, if your partner stays in hospital afterwards, she may find it tricky to sleep when the air is filled with the faint sounds of babies crying and the woman in the bed next door is shrieking at her contractions every two minutes.

There won't be any *Die Hard*.

At the end of the day, it's all about what's best for mum and baby, and what you're all happy with as a family. Just make sure you do your prep, talk through your options, and make your decision in good time. And hey, if you do opt for a hospital birth, *Die Hard* is repeated on TV all the time, so it's not like you'll have to wait long.

Sources Used
Home Birth Reference Site
http://www.homebirth.org.uk/

Chamberlain, Wraight and Crowley; *Home Births: The Report of the 1994 Confidential Enquiry by the National Birthday Trust Fund*

DECISIONS: DISPOSABLE OR REUSABLE

I'm talking about nappies, of course. Although your partner could possibly be described as disposable and reusable, I don't think the world would take too kindly to me listing the pros and cons of each. So yes, nappies.

Tree-huggers – sorry, I mean those who are 'environmentally friendly' – will herald reusable nappies as a great way to save money and the environment. Those who reckon disposable nappies are the mutt's nuts will point to the fact that when you're out and about it's dead easy to lob a dirty nappy in the bin as opposed to having one stuffed into the corner of a bag, making your debit card smell like poo.

So which is better? As with the other 'Decisions' chapters, I'm not here to make your mind up for you. All I can give you are the pros and cons of each. So here we go:

REUSABLE NAPPIES

Advantages

- The environment loves you. Instead of disposable nappies being lobbed into a landfill to take hundreds of years to decay, reusable nappies are – surprisingly – reusable.

- Reusable nappies do not contain any potentially harmful chemicals or gels, like disposable nappies. Therefore, you know what is coming into contact with your baby's skin.
- Whilst perhaps stinking a bit beforehand, reusable nappies are easy to clean. Just lob them into a bucket lined with a mesh bag, then stick the bag into the washing machine at 40 or 60 degrees Celsius, and Bob's your uncle.

Bob.

- When you think reusable nappies, those big towel things come to mind, held together by a massive safety pin. That's not the case any more, and reusable nappies have been better designed to limit the restriction of baby movement.
- Because you are reusing nappies and not shelling out the best part of a tenner a time on disposables, your bank balance will look much better in the long-term.

Disadvantages

- You'll have to purchase all the supplies up front and at once, which can cost a few hundred quid. There is also an element of ongoing cost, when buying new nappy insert cloths, that kind of thing.
- Perhaps not so environmentally-friendly, you'll need to put on an extra load of washing once every two or three days. This could result in an increase in your utility bills.
- Whilst not half as bad as they were, some reusable nappies are still pretty bulky, and might go some way to limiting movement. They also make your baby look like he or she has a 'bootay', which I'm told is youth speak for 'massive arse'.
- The absorption qualities of a reusable nappy might be a bit limited, which could cause nappy rash and a generally cranky baby if you're not able to immediately change him or her.
- There is a specific way of putting a reusable nappy together; you have to fold the cloth and put a liner around it before you can even think about sticking it on your baby. This can take a bit of getting used to.

DISPOSABLE NAPPIES

Advantages

- Probably the biggest advantage of disposable nappies is their convenience. If your baby does a massive dump while you're out and about, you can just whip off the nappy and slam dunk it into the nearest bin without worrying about how you're going to get it home.
- Disposable nappies are well designed to allow full baby movement, and - as technology advances - are becoming better at absorbing liquids to keep your baby dry.
- You don't need to worry about putting extra loads of washing on.
- Disposable nappies are pretty easy to use; just a couple of tabs, stick 'em down, job done.
- Many shops, including some service stations, will stock disposable nappies; so if you run out, you don't need to freak out too much.

Disadvantages

- The biggest disadvantage is cost. Over time, buying packs of nappies can cost a small fortune, which leaves less beer money for you. Research shows that a child who is in nappies for two and a half years will use around 6,000 disposable nappies.
- Disposable nappies contain a number of chemicals, whose job it is to absorb liquids. There's a risk, albeit small, that these

chemicals can come into contact with your baby's skin, causing burns.

- The environment does not love you. Whilst some nappies are 'bio-friendly', meaning they decay quicker than others, many are still sent to landfill sites, making this green and pleasant land look markedly browner.

Bottom line is, your baby is going to poo whether you go for reusable or disposable nappies. The choice, good sir, is yours.

Sources Used
The Nappy Lady: Advice
http://www.thenappylady.co.uk/public/advice.aspx

Babykind: Why Choose Reusable Nappies?
http://www.babykind.co.uk/whychoosereusables.htm

BBC Health: Nappies
http://www.bbc.co.uk/health/physical_health/child_developmen
t/newborn_nappies.shtml

DECISIONS: PAIN RELIEF DURING LABOUR

"GIMME THE DRUGS!!" screams your partner, her spittle peppering your face as she grabs your collar and pulls you towards her. From this distance, you can see the bulging veins in her forehead, the manic look in her eyes, and that sense of impending crotch-crushing if you don't do exactly what she says right there, right then.

Now would probably be the wrong time to gently explain to her the different pain relief options she has, some of them not involving drugs at all. This suggestion would definitely be met with a swipe at your face and a perhaps not-so-polite repeat of her request for drugs.

There's no right or wrong pain relief during labour; every woman has a different pain threshold. Some may opt for an epidural straight away, some may try to do the whole thing without drugs at all. With both our boys, Jess had just a TENS machine – but that's only because by the time she'd reached the point where she wanted drugs it was too late.

Pain relief can be categorised under two headings: non-drugs, and drugs. Imaginative, I know.

Non-Drug Pain Relief

If you and your partner would rather not opt for pain relief medication, there are a number of things you can do to ease any discomfort. Unfortunately, these techniques are just for the mother. You're going to have to sort yourself out some other way, you blubbering wreck.

Massage

Massage can be a simple yet effective way of relieving pain, if done properly. The crucial word there is 'properly'. Randomly pinching her shoulders or doing those little karate chops on her back are going to do little or nothing to help the situation. Imagine doing that to a tiger, and you'll get some idea of what will happen if you don't massage properly.

Lower back massage is pretty helpful. Put your hands either side of her spine at the base of her back whilst she kneels on the floor, or on all fours. Make sure they are just above her bumcrack, in what's known as the sacral region. Then, when she has a contraction, push your hands up to her waist level, making sure you don't massage directly over the spine. Then, sit back and dust yourself off, you stud.

Breathing Exercises

You may have learnt these during antenatal classes, and carrying out breathing exercises can help your mrs relax, lowering the amount of pain she's in. You can also breathe, if you so wish.

Hypnobirthing

Hypnobirthing basically involves teaching the mother how to control her thought processes during labour to keep her positive and manage her pain. As if your 'you can do it' dance and fist-pumping isn't enough.

Acupuncture

Strategically placed needles in ear points are attached to electrodes, which administer mild stimulation, which she'd probably be used to with you. Mild. Ha!

A quick note – make sure the needles are administered by a qualified therapist. Using your wife as a human Voodoo doll will not go down well, despite taking her mind off the contractions.

TENS Machine

Full name Transcutaneous Electrical Nerve Stimulation, a TENS machine sends weak electrical pulses through pads placed on the back, interfering with the pain signals and preventing them from reaching your mrs' brain. They're pretty inexpensive, and your partner – or you, if she's foolish – can control the strength of the pulses. Not to be used in water, obviously.

Water

Taking a dip in water that does not exceed 37°C can help soothe pain and relax the mum. You have to be careful that you don't use this method too early, though, as it can slow labour down. Your mrs should be at least 5cm dilated before she uses a pool. You may or may not (probably not) wish to get in with her, but you will be given a net with which to scoop out any little brown fish.

Pain Relief Using Drugs

Sometimes, these 'natural' pain relieving methods just aren't enough, in which case those good ol' drugs are called upon to go about their business.

Entonox (Gas and Air)

This is a mixture of half oxygen and half nitrous oxide – otherwise known as laughing gas. Fortunately or unfortunately, depending upon how you look at it, the laughing gas ratio isn't enough to turn your mrs into a whooping, thigh-slapping, tears-rolling-down-her-cheeks clown, and she still won't laugh at your jokes.

Gas and air has a calming effect without causing excessive drowsiness, the pain relief kicking in after around 30 to 45 seconds. It does not remain in the mother's system after it's been used, and won't affect your baby at all.

There are a few side effects that the mother can experience, such as light-headedness or nausea, but to be honest my mrs gets those symptoms every time she looks at me.

Pethidine, Diamorphine, Meptazinol

No, those aren't suggestions for baby names, although that would be pretty cool. These are pain-killing injections, which have an effect almost instantly and last for two to three hours. Because they can often cause nausea, the mum will also be given an anti-emetic, which will stop her from vomming everywhere.

Pain relief is only limited, but the advantage is that labour is not slowed down at all. However, if given in large doses, or too close to the delivery of the baby, both baby and mum can become drowsy. This can have a knock-on effect in delaying successful breastfeeding, and in some cases – where the drug crosses the placenta – your baby can be drowsy for several days. You'll be drowsy, too – but that's because you'll have had about three hours sleep.

Epidural

Epidurals are becoming increasingly common during labour. Administered directly into the space around the spinal cord, an epidural numbs the nerves that transport pain to the brain. A tube will often be left in your partner's back to administer top ups as and when required.

Epidurals are only normally used during the latter stages of labour, when contractions are really starting to cause serious pain. You can't fault the pain relief; a herd of bulls could trample over your mrs' legs and she wouldn't feel a thing, although she would still have a clear mind so would be a tad freaked out. Also, you'd have to question why you were sharing your delivery room/living room with a herd of bulls.

It's a pretty complicated procedure, though, taking 20 minutes to set up and another 20 to take full effect. Your mrs will be pretty much tethered to the bed, and as such won't be able to get up and walk around if she wants to. It can also slow down labour, as the mother is depending upon the midwives to tell her when to push.

There is a higher risk of assisted delivery, such as the use of forceps, and maybe even a Caesarean section in extreme cases.

That's pretty much pain relief in a nutshell; and it's up to you to decide, like a contestant on *Who Wants To Be A Millionaire?* only without the prospect of winning a shedload of money at the end of it.

Sources Used
NHS: Pain Relief During Labour and Birth
http://www.nhs.uk/livewell/pregnancy/Pages/Painrelief.aspx

Babycentre: Pain Relief During Labour
http://www.babycentre.co.uk/pregnancy/labourandbirth/painreli
ef/

HOW TO:
CHOOSE A BABY NAME

Apart from just how you're going to avoid getting your face burnt off by your hormonal partner, choosing your baby's name is one of the most difficult decisions for you both to make; and even if you're both lucky enough to decide on a name relatively quickly, the last thing you want is to look it up on the interweb only to find it means 'minger' in German. So, here are some things you need to consider when choosing a moniker for your child. Also, Ben is an awesome name. Just sayin'.

"Hello, my name's Quentin. I'm 35 and have never been kissed."

Unless your child goes through the relevant legal processes, the name you give them is for life. That means that popular names now might be pretty awful decades into the future. I mean, can you imagine calling a child Mabel? Perhaps, but only if it had a moustache and boiled sweets in its nappy.

If you get caught up in choosing an unusual name – which is not a problem in itself at all, goodness knows there's far too many Johns in the world – just think about how you'd like to be called that name. Whilst Cobra sounds pretty cool, you're not a Gladiator, and never will be. What if your kid grows up to be weedy? A name like Hulk will just seem daft.

Check out the most popular names

There are tonnes of websites around that will tell you the most popular names for boys and girls in the last few years, and these may provide a bit of inspiration if you're chewing the heck out of your pencil trying to think of a decent name.

A tip: check popular dog and cat names too, to make sure your child won't share their name with a thousand Labradors. Apparently, Ben is a pretty common dog name, which perhaps explains why I really like chasing sticks and peeing against trees.

"You have my ex-girlfriend's eyes..."

Bear in mind that your favourite name might hold bad memories for your other half, especially if you land on a name belonging to an ex. The last thing you want each time you call your kid down from his bedroom is for your partner to feel seething anger at some guy who didn't take her to the prom fifteen years previously, and then had the cheek to make out with Kirsty McShay beside the tables of non-alcoholic champagne whilst she watched on, all panda-eyed and snotty.

Let's just call him Archie

A good tip to remember is that long forenames go well with short surnames, and vice versa. If you are blessed with a twelve-syllable surname and you give your kid a six-syllable first name, you run the risk of every school teacher he or she ever has suffering from an asthma attack during class registration each day just trying to get the words out. Similarly, if your child has a couple of two-syllable names it'll sound like Morse code every time you shout it.

A name that is too long can reduce a once-proud pencil to a mere stub.

And I know it's cliché, but make sure you say full names out loud before you finally decide. Your child will hate you forever if you make the classic mistake of calling it Ben Dover, Dwayne Pipe, or Sandy Ramsbottom – although, if you're unfortunate enough to have Ramsbottom as a surname, I'd probably go to the trouble of getting it changed.

"That's got a 'I' on the end, not a 'Y'. 'I'. No, 'I'."

It's commonplace to slightly alter the spelling of a name to make it more modern, sticking an 'I' on the end instead of a 'Y', or something; and as this intelligently titled section implies, your poor kid is probably going to spend a lifetime spelling it out to people.

Finally, think about the initials you're giving your child. As soon as your kid's mates realise that his or her initials spell 'ASS' or 'BUM' they'll be on it like a shot, and your kid might come home and punch you in the crotch for giving him such a sucky name.

And he'll be wearing one of these.

HOW TO:
PACK A HOSPITAL BAG

I'll tell you something for free, because I'm nice like that: when your mrs gets her first contraction and begins to panic, the last thing she's going to want is

 you legging it round the house in your underwear frantically stuffing everything you can lay your hands on into a bag for the hospital. It's recommended that you pack the bag around week 36; then, you can calmly pick up the bag and guide your partner to the car, giving off an aura of serenity whilst you poo your pants in secret.

So here's what needs to go in the hospital bags, to make sure your baby doesn't spend its first days swaddled in a carrier bag from Asda. Note I've changed it to 'bags', although you may want to stuff it all into one big bag. You'll need different things for during and after the birth, though, so it's up to you.

The Bag for Labour

Here's what you and your partner will need for labour and childbirth:

- **Maternity Notes**
- **Birth Plan**

- **Old clothes** (baggy T-shirt, scabby pyjamas, that kind of thing; basically, anything that she doesn't mind being spattered in goo.)
- **TENS Machine:** Hospitals only have a limited number of TENS machines, so you might want to take your own. They cost around £30-£40 for a good one.
- **Books/Magazines:** For those times when labour lasts for days. Pornography will probably be frowned upon by the hospital staff and patients (remember, you'll be surrounded by women).
- **Food and Drink:** Food high in energy is best, such as cereal bars. Same with the drink: take an isotonic sports drink or something similar. No beers.
- **Camera:** For those first photos of your baby. Beware: photos showing crowning or afterbirth do not go well on the front of an announcement card.
- **Music:** Many delivery rooms have a CD player, or you can take an MP3 player with your partner's favourite thrash metal on it.
- **Toiletries:** Deodorant, face wipes, that kind of thing. Anything that'll help her look normal whilst squeezing out a baby. Some sources suggest packing a water spray to keep her cool, but – like a cat – she might just think you're telling her off.
- **Phone Numbers:** Imagine how crushed your mum would be if everyone else knew about the baby's arrival before her. You horrible man. Get a list of phone numbers in priority order so you can tell everyone who needs to know in person.

The Post-Birth Bag — For Mum

I refrained from calling it the 'Afterbirth' bag, as that would imply that you'll be taking the placenta home with you. Which you might. But that's weird.

- **Change of clothes:** For leaving the hospital. The sight of your mrs walking across the car park like she has a broom up her bum - and with various stains all over her clothes - might alert hospital security staff.
- **Nursing Bras:** The ones with the cups that detach so your mrs can breastfeed, if that's what you've decided to do.
- **Breast Pads:** To absorb any leaks. These are for her only, I should add. The chances of you leaking are pretty much zero.
- **Maternity Pads and Underwear:** Women continue to bleed after birth, so get some pads on the go.
- **Toiletries:** Hairbrush, deodorant, face wipes, perhaps a bit of make up; whatever allows your partner to put her face back on and stop looking like the Joker.

The Post-Birth Bag — For Baby

No deodorant required, although lipstick would look kinda cool.

- **Clothing:** Onesies, babygrows, vests, and an outfit for their first trip home.
- **Muslin Squares:** For wiping up dribble and puke (really meant just for baby, but you can use one for yourself if needs be).

- **Cotton Wool Balls:** Best for washing baby's skin when changing their nappy for the first few weeks.
- **Nappies:** Otherwise your kid will poo over anything and everything, as well as spraying a neat arc of pee across a foot radius (if it's a boy, that is).
- **Nappy Sacks**
- **Blanket**

And don't forget: fix the car seat in your car before the due date so you can actually take your baby home from the hospital. Make sure it's regulation, legal, and fitted correctly; strapping your child to the roof is almost definitely illegal.

HOW TO:
CREATE A BIRTH PLAN

A plan for birth? Out of that hole there would be a good start. (Cue lingering point)

Unfortunately, birth plans are a bit more detailed than that, and although they aren't compulsory, they can certainly help inform your midwife as to what drugs your mrs wants, who she wants in the room, that kind of thing. Although the request as to who she would like in the room is somewhat limited; Brad Pitt is unlikely to pull himself away from his next blockbuster to watch the partner of someone he doesn't even know wail in agony, even if he does get his hand held throughout.

A birth plan covers a number of aspects, from what your stance is on Caesarean sections right down to the music you may want playing in the background. By the way, with the music thing, can I suggest a bit of Salt-N-Pepa. I just think the sound of "aah-sshh push it" bouncing off the walls in time with your mrs' contractions would just add a comical tinge to events.

The thing is, no matter how detailed you make a birth plan, you can't see the future; and complications might arise during labour that means your birth plan ends up lying on the tarmac outside in a little screwed-up ball, and Plan B implemented. (Which isn't to just panic, by the way. That doesn't really help anything.)

When do we write a birth plan?

You can write a birth plan pretty much anytime before your baby is born; any time afterwards, and it becomes a bit of a waste of time. Ideally, you're looking at six to eight weeks before the due date to draw up a plan, as you might want to give a copy to your midwife so that she can read through it and let you know if there's any issues. Make sure it's brief, as well. Your midwife won't be happy if a 100-page dossier is lobbed onto her lap as your mrs dilates another centimetre.

What goes into a birth plan?

Here's an idea of just a few things that would go into your average birth plan. The whole point of a birth plan is that you both get to make these decisions, so don't just sit back and let your mrs forge ahead.

Birth Companion

This is basically who gets the delight of being there when your baby is born. Some parents who are opting for a home birth may want their kids there, others may want friends or family members there –

whether they're giving birth at home or in the hospital.

You may have opted for a doula (a professional birth partner), and they'd obviously need to be there, otherwise you're paying them for sitting around in a corridor. This part of the birth plan also needs to tell the midwife whether you want this little gaggle of observers there for the whole time, or if you'd like them to leave once the baby starts crowning away. Whether or not they applaud once your child finally slips out is entirely up to them.

Special Needs

If the mother is disabled, or has any other special needs, then list them here. This will allow the midwife to act accordingly to make sure that the whole experience goes as smoothly as possible. Any dietary or religious requirements get listed here as well, although I doubt your mrs will be chomping on a steak as she contracts every two minutes. You, on the other hand, can eat what you want, because you're awesome.

Positioning

Some mothers want to be as active as possible during labour, wandering around and giving a little wiggle every now and then in the hope that the baby will just fall out; others may be happier bed-bound. Your partner may also want to deliver the baby in a different position than the classic on-the-back pose, such as squatting or on all fours.

Birthing Pool

Some midwives might suggest a birthing pool, either as a form of pain relief or to facilitate a water birth. Let the midwife know either  way what you would both prefer. Although you can, I would refrain from jumping into the pool with her, because after a while that water's going to get murky.

Pain Relief

Perhaps one of the most important parts of the birth plan, the pain relief section will detail which drugs you do and don't want for your partner. The birth plan will also list in what order you would like the drugs to be administered. Writing 'epidural' for your top three isn't really that helpful, although it gets the point across.

After the Birth

Your partner may want skin-to-skin contact immediately after birth, before your baby has been washed. Fortunately, although your baby will be gooey, it won't be like trying to hold a wet bar of soap.

You may also want to cut the cord, or decide that you'd like another birthing partner to do this. Make sure the midwife knows about this, as they tend to go into robot mode once the baby's born and may do it themselves without realising.

Vitamin K

Approximately 1 in 10,000 babies in the UK are born with a vitamin K deficiency, which can result in death. All babies are offered a vitamin K injection straight after birth, which eliminates this risk. You should write on your birth plan whether you do or do not want this injection to be administered.

Placenta

The mum is always offered an injection after birth to help speed up the delivery of the placenta. If you'd rather it be delivered naturally, then note this on your birth plan.

Some parents may also want to keep the placenta, to bury it or do something else with it, depending upon what they believe in. They may also just fancy a placenta sandwich.

Complications

Sometimes, there are complications, and your baby may have to be delivered using forceps, ventouse or a C-section. Make sure you decide before birth what you do and don't want and make sure it's written down.

Student Doctors/Midwives

You may or may not feel comfortable with a spotty student gawping at your partner during labour, or maybe even getting a bit involved with stitches and the like. Either way, let the midwife know.

As well as letting the midwife know the decisions that you've made, having the chat with your partner before the due date will give you a good chance to talk through any concerns and do a bit of research on all your options. It'll also allow you to fight your mrs' corner if she gets too exhausted or distressed during birth to do so herself. And by fight, I mean verbally. Landing a sweet Superman punch on a midwife or doctor will probably not go down too well.

HOW TO:
BE A GREAT BIRTHING PARTNER

Rocking gently in the corner with your knees by your chin as your partner squeezes out your baby is not a good look. Whether she puts on a brave face or not, your mrs is going to need you for support and encouragement before, during and after labour. We've come a long way since the middle of last century, where dads weren't allowed in the delivery room and remained as distant throughout the child's life; we're face deep in fatherhood now, and even if you get scared, nervous or weepy during the moment when your baby arrives, you need to make sure that you're there for the mum as much as you can be.

However, it should be said at the outset that this is a highly charged time, and – for some dads – it can all be a bit too much. If you're one of those dads, then relax. Not being physically present at the birth won't damage your father-child bond, or your bond with your partner. Being a man means knowing your own limits.

Let's go on: your role as the birth partner does not begin with the first contraction and end when the cord is cut. You've got to be there before, during and after, getting stuff done so the big day goes as smoothly as possible. That's right, stuff done; so get your hand out of your waistband, quit watching TV and get off your bum.

Before the Big Day

You don't need me to tell you that you need to do a fair bit of preparation for labour. If you don't, you put yourself at risk of standing next to a car that's run out of petrol on the side of a dark country road, shrugging uselessly as your partner panics between contractions on the back seat. You'll wish you're in a soap opera. Babies are born without the hassle of an umbilical cord in soap operas.

One of the first things to do is get a birth plan drawn up. It'll help you decide what kind of pain relief you want, who you want at the birth, that kind of thing – and will give the midwife handy info so she doesn't keep pestering you for answers.

Whether you're having a home birth or a hospital birth, it's a good idea to get a bag packed in good time, full of things like toiletries, food, drinks, and a change of clothing. Get some stuff in there for yourself as well, because if it's a long labour you could end up being so hungry you chew on your own arm, which would cause a headache for the doctors.

Although you might get an awesome replacement.

It's also a good idea to prepare a phone list of friends and family who you'd like to ring once your baby's arrived. This is also a handy way of making sure you've remembered everyone: nothing says 'family rejection' like forgetting to tell your dad that he's now a granddad, and him finding out from the hairdresser instead.

Make sure your car has a full fuel tank. Even though you're a man, and yes, you've got big muscles, you're not going to be able to push your car to the local hospital if it starts coughing and spluttering on the way. Similarly, waiting in the queue to pay at a petrol station whilst your mrs claws at the dashboard in pain isn't going to go down too well. Even if you're planning a home birth, make sure you've got enough in the tank in case of complications or a last-minute change of plan.

Finally, get the food in, specifically energy bars and food high in carbs. Your mrs will need these to muster up the energy to give birth; fruit juices are also a good tip. Roast dinners, despite being tasty, aren't all that practical.

During the Big Day

Labour day is a highly charged time, and you can be easily forgiven for being a bit overwhelmed and queasy – indeed, some dads might find the experience so emotive that they can't stay with the mother whilst she is giving birth; and that's fine. While she may miss your support, she'll have one or two midwives with her who will give her all the direction and encouragement she needs.

For those dads who are able to stick it out, it's important that you remain focussed and calm. The midwives are not going to be best pleased if they keep having to scrape you off the floor when they should be monitoring the baby's heartbeat, or trying to convince the mum to move around a bit.

There may also be times where your partner will need you to stand up for her. Your midwife will have the birth plan, and it is up to you to reinforce what you as a couple have decided, unless it will put the mum at risk. In the throes of labour, your mrs may not be able to communicate very well with the midwives – at least not in a calm, non-screaming fashion – and so she'll be relying upon you to make sure that she gets the treatment she wants.

"PETHIDIIIIINE!"

She'll also need you to provide encouragement, the odd pep talk when things perhaps get a bit tough. We're talking gentle words of encouragement here, not some kind of American Football half-time tongue-lashing from a big red-faced manager, telling her to "get out there and get the job done, you inbred!" That won't help. Be there for her, keep her spirits up and make sure you tell her how well she's doing. As much as we may indulge in a little light mockery, the fact is we will never experience anything like this, and so cannot possibly judge. Encourage and motivate your mrs during this pretty scary time – and make eye contact. Looking at your toes and muttering "yeah, keep it up" isn't going to help. Instead, looking her in the eyes will promote trust and care, and allow the mum to refocus, safe in the knowledge that you're there to claw if needs be.

You also play the role of waiter, giving the mum food and drink as and when needed, as well as the odd cold flannel on the forehead. It's your job to make her feel as comfortable as possible, which also extends to suggesting alternative labour positions if she's in a lot of pain as she is.

Essentially, your job is to be there. This is a big deal for you as well, of course – but at this moment you need to put your own worries aside and concentrate on keeping the mum going.

After the Big Day

If you have chosen a doula to help during childbirth, making regular post-natal checks should be part of her remit. You'll also get appearances from health visitors, who will check over mum and baby and make sure they're OK – so your role after birth changes slightly.

Firstly, you're going to get a lot of requests from family and friends to see the baby. Whilst their intentions are good, you need some time with your little boy or girl to bond with them, and chill out after a manic day or so. Some people will even turn up unannounced to visit, which should be a slappable offence.

In hospital there are set waiting times, and so it's not so bad – but when mum and baby come home for the first time your job is to act as gatekeeper, to try and limit the almost endless flow of visitors. The mum will no doubt be tired, and you might be pretty knackered too – and so having grannies incessantly ticking the underside of your baby's chin can wear a bit thin after a while. A good tip is to set aside just one or two days a week for visitors, leaving the remaining time for rest and family bonding.

Chances are your mrs won't be immediately mobile enough to make you a sandwich, and so it's down to you to provide food for the family. It's always wise in the weeks leading up to the birth to stock up on frozen meals for those crazy first few days with your little one. They're quick and easy, and don't leave a massive amount of washing up.

Talking of washing up, it's your job to don the apron and get to work carrying out the household chores, making sure that everywhere is clean and tidy. Your mrs isn't going to feel like wading through a knee-high sea of your dirty boxers just to get to the loo.

Basically, your post-birth role is all about getting involved, assisting where possible, even just being there to listen to her. Oh – and getting up in the middle of the night to get stuck in to another pooey nappy.

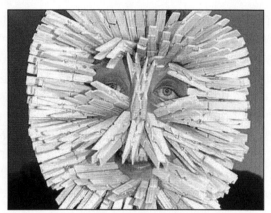
Yeah, just the one peg will suffice.

HOW TO:
MINIMISE THE RISK OF COT DEATH

The purpose of this chapter is not to scare you. I'm not going to blind you with statistics about how many babies die of cot death, or 'Sudden Infant Death Syndrome' as it is often called. Needless to say, it sometimes – and, very tragically – happens. It's not been fully established what causes it: it could be an infection, a defect the baby's always had; even gases emitted from baby mattresses have been mooted as the cause for SIDS. But there are ways in which you can help prevent cot death.

Smoking

It has been proven that exposure to cigarette smoke, both during pregnancy and after birth, is known to increase the risk of cot death. Therefore, don't do it. If you or someone has to smoke, then do it outside.

Sleeping

The best place for your baby to sleep for the first six months is in your room. Whilst this might give you a rough night, as you wake up every time it sniffs – it'll help put your mind at rest.

There are a few tips to take on board when putting your baby down to sleep:

- Lie the baby on its back.

- Place your baby with its feet at the foot of the cot. This will stop it from squirming under any blankets or covers.
- Do not fall asleep holding your baby.
- Don't use a pillow in your baby's cot.
- Use a firm mattress, and one with a waterproof cover.
- Do not leave blankets loose; instead, tuck them in to make them secure.
- Never cover your baby's head.

Some resources recommend that you only share a bed with your baby if it is older than three months. Whether you share your bed with your baby is your choice, but never do so if you've been drinking or taking medication that makes you drowsy.

Temperature

Keeping your baby at the right temperature (between 16 to 20°C) is very important, and a good reason for buying one of those thermometers that you stick onto the wall.

Again, some tips:

- Don't check your baby's temperature by feeling its forehead; instead, feel the stomach or chest instead.
- Remove outdoor clothes when you go inside.
- Don't let your baby sleep in direct sunlight, next to a radiator, or with a hot water bottle.
- Do not use duvets until your baby is more than a year old.

- Baby sleeping bags are great; but make sure you buy one that is a suitable Tog rating for the room temperature. It's probably a good idea to buy a few bags with different thicknesses.

Sources Used

BUPA: Cot death and sudden infant death syndrome (SIDS)
http://hcd2.bupa.co.uk/fact_sheets/html/sids.html#3

Foundation for the Study of Infant Deaths
http://fsid.org.uk

HOW TO:
BURP A BABY

So, you've fed your baby. That sentence assumes you've been bottle feeding, otherwise you – as a father – have a remarkable gift, and should probably go on TV. Now you need to burp it, and this is where things either get messy, or you're sat there for hours patting away to no avail.

Please don't ask me how I got my hands on this photo.

What's the point of making your baby burp anyway? I mean yeah, it's cute, and people react well to babies burping for some reason. Unfortunately, this kind of reaction is reversed when you're older: if I was to burp now, for example, just sat at this computer, I would get an evil look, perhaps a tut, and more than likely a bit of quicksick. Fortunately, the sympathetic reactions come back the older you get. Have you ever seen how people respond to pensioners farting? It's like they've just seen a kitten with blowdried fur looking all sweet and fuzzy.

But anyway, the point of burping: if you don't burp your baby, it could get trapped wind. His or her digestive system isn't as advanced as us adults, and gas can easily build up and cause discomfort; not just for your baby, but for you, as you get up every ten minutes to see to a shrieking child. It can also cause the child to do what the Americans call 'spitting up', where it regurgitates a little bit of bubbly milk, making it look like your child has rabies. We in the UK call it 'puking'. Just so you know.

Let's get to the crux of this matter, instead of talking about farting pensioners and babies with rabies. There are three main ways to burp a baby. This should not be tried on pensioners. It's demeaning.

Method One: Over the Shoulder
1. Put a muslin square or cloth over your shoulder. The last thing you want is baby vom on your new shirt.
2. Hold your baby over your shoulder so his head is resting just above your collarbone with his stomach facing your chest.
3. Pat your baby's back gently or rub in a slow circular motion until he belches in your ear.

Method Two: The Bulldog Burp
So called because the way you cradle your baby's face makes it look all wrinkly like a bulldog. It has nothing to do with stubby legs or a little tail.

1. Sit your baby on your lap, and place your hand on his chest.

2. Gently cradle his chin with the crook between your finger and thumb and lean him forward onto your hand.
3. With the other, do the whole patting and rubbing thing.

Method Three: Across the Lap

1. Lie your baby across your lap so his head is on one thigh and his stomach on the other.
2. Make sure his cheek is on your thigh. As well as ensuring your baby doesn't suffocate, it means you won't get your trousers gummed by a confused child.
3. Pat and rub until you hear that sweet burping sound.

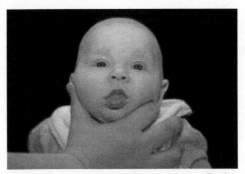

"This could be a burp or puke. I'm not going to lie, it could go either way."

HOW TO:
MAKE A PLACENTA SHAKE

Some people are a bit weird, and decide to actually do stuff with the placenta once it's been delivered, instead of being like everyone else and simply chucking it away. It has been linked to minimising the risk of postpartum depression, but instead of eating your own placenta I would suggest simply watching a funny movie and eating chocolate.

So some people eat it - perhaps laying it on toast as a handy snack - and some people drink it, blending it up and mixing it with something to hide the grossness. Some people even use it as a small pillow. (They don't, really. I made that up). However, some people do make placenta prints. I'm not one to judge, but those people are freakin' weird.

Google 'eat placenta'. Go on, I dare you.

Anyway; here's how to make a placenta shake, if you so desire (courtesy of eHow.com, with a few pointless and vaguely funny bits added by me):

Ingredients

Placenta
Four strawberries
A handful of blueberries
½ cup of milk
Two capfuls of acidophilus
Maple Syrup
Ice cubes

Instructions

1. Trim a piece off the placenta about the size of your thumb, but make sure you at least attempt to cuddle your baby first. The midwife will be a bit puzzled if you run into the kitchen clutching the placenta and giggling.
2. Wash the strawberries and blueberries.
3. Put the placenta and fruit in a blender along with the milk, acidophilus, maple syrup and 3 to 4 ice cubes.
4. Blend until you forget that you just put placenta in your blender.
5. The results will provide about a glass and a half of shake. Holding your nose as you down it is optional, but encouraged.

A LETTER TO MY UNBORN FOETUS

Dear Foetus-Face,

I call you that not out of nastiness, instead purely because I want to make sure that you look like the name we've chosen for you before I use it. It may be that when we see you for the first time, our name might not suit you. I'm sincerely hoping that when you come sliding out of your mother, you don't look like a Leroy, or a Mohammed, or a Dim Sum-Choi. If you do, me and your mum will be having a few choice words as she expels the placenta that's been feeding you for the last nine months.

Just on the whole delivery thing: try not to give your mum too much grief on the way out. Don't do anything daft like stretch out your arms, or dig yourself in so labour lasts for days. I'm the one that'll bear the brunt of her anguish, and if I do I'll have no qualms with smoking you out or taking a pair of BBQ tongs to you in an effort to get things over and done with. I'll even use the vacuum cleaner if I have to, you just try me.

I have to say: I'm very excited to meet you. I kind of hope I don't cry when I see you for the first time; I've spent over two decades building up an image, and I don't want that ruined as I sob into the bosom of an uncomfortable midwife. But I can't wait to see what you look like, whether you have the same eyes as your mum (I hope so) or the same nose as me (I hope not). If you're lucky, you'll get the best features from both of us. If not: well, sorry about that.

I promise I'll get up when you cry during the night, although it's your mother who has the food hanging from her chest, so I don't know how much use I'll be. I promise I'll wait a few years before we wrestle for the first time; for my own sake more than yours. The prospect of being pinned to the floor by a child who can't even lift his own head is very real, and not one that I want to risk happening. I promise I won't give up after half an hour of trying to make you burp, and I really won't mind if you need me to rock you to sleep at 2am.

Once you're old enough, I'll take you and your brother to football and rugby matches, and disown you if you want to see the ballet instead. I'll kiss your knees when you fall over in the garden, and — until you get too heavy — I'll happily walk around town with you on my shoulders.

No doubt I'll get grumpy with you when you demand more food, or if you pester me when I'm working. But rest assured, I will always love you and make sure that I tell you so every day. I'll come into your room at night and give you a kiss on the forehead, and — whether you like it or not — this will probably continue until you leave home in your mid-teens. Get used to it.

A warning: there will be many, many times when I embarrass you in public, especially in front of your friends. When you get your first girlfriend, I'll undoubtedly say something that will make her run a mile. Again, sorry about that. You'll learn to tune me out after a few years, I'm sure.

Anyway, I have to go. You're kicking your mother's insides to smithereens and I have to make her yet another cup of tea.

See you soon, little guy. Can't wait to meet you.

Loads of love, kisses, and the occasional manly handshake,

Your Dad

x

WHY NURSERY RHYMES ARE EVIL

Jack and Jill

Jack and Jill went up the hill
To fetch a pail of water.
Jack fell down and bumped his crown
And Jill came tumbling after.

Firstly, this nursery rhyme is stupid because it has no moral. It barely has a storyline. Two kids go up a hill to get some water, end up falling back down, one of them suffering serious head traumas. Sleep tight, son.

Humpty Dumpty

Humpty Dumpty sat on a wall
Humpty Dumpty had a great fall.
All the king's horses and all the king's men
Couldn't put Humpty together again.

It's no surprise that the horses were unable to put Humpty together again. Firstly, their hooves are not conducive to holding surgical tools. Secondly, they'd struggle to get masks that would cover their big faces properly.

This rhyme would benefit from a second verse, as it's pretty open-ended. What happened next? Did all the king's horses and all the king's men just leave him there, at the foot of the wall, in a broken state? 'Cos that's just mean.

There was an old lady who swallowed a fly...

There was an old lady who swallowed a fly
I don't know why she swallowed a fly - perhaps
she'll die!
There was an old lady who swallowed a spider,
That wriggled and wiggled and tiggled inside her;
She swallowed the spider to catch the fly;
I don't know why she swallowed a fly - Perhaps
she'll die!
There was an old lady who swallowed a bird;
How absurd to swallow a bird.
She swallowed the bird to catch the spider,
She swallowed the spider to catch the fly;
I don't know why she swallowed a fly - Perhaps
she'll die!

...

There was an old lady who swallowed a cow,
I don't know how she swallowed a cow;
She swallowed the cow to catch the dog,
She swallowed the dog to catch the cat,
She swallowed the cat to catch the bird,
She swallowed the bird to catch the spider,
She swallowed the spider to catch the fly;
I don't know why she swallowed a fly - Perhaps
she'll die!
There was an old lady who swallowed a horse...
She's dead, of course!

This rhyme is just screwed up beyond belief. Of course the woman died when she ate the horse. It's a wonder she got past the cat without severe digestive issues.

One, Two, Three Four Five...

One, two, three four five
Once I caught a fish alive.
Six, seven, eight nine ten
Then I let it go again.

Why did you let it go?
Because it bit my finger so.
Which finger did it bite?
This little finger on my right.

What they don't tell you is, that fish was a freakin' Great White. And it came back later for more fisherman meat.

Three Blind Mice

Three blind mice
Three blind mice
See how they run
See how they run
They all ran after the farmer's wife
She cut off their tails with a carving knife
Did you ever see such a sight in your life
As three blind mice?

Not only do these poor handicapped rodents have to stumble through life with no eyesight, some horrid woman in an apron slices off their tails, and with it their sense of balance. Now they're just wobbly mice who are constantly feeling for obstacles. Their career prospects are, at best, grim.

Oranges and Lemons

"Oranges and lemons" say the Bells of St.
Clement's
"You owe me five farthings" say the Bells of St.
Martin's
"When will you pay me?" say the Bells of Old Bailey
"When I grow rich" say the Bells of Shoreditch
"When will that be?" say the Bells of Stepney
"I do not know" say the Great Bells of Bow
"Here comes a candle to light you to bed
And here comes a chopper to chop off your head.

This particular ditty gave me nightmares until I was 18. It makes little sense, and then tells you that someone's coming to chop off your head. What do you mean, you can't sleep?

Rock a Bye Baby

Rock a bye baby on the tree top
When the wind blows, the cradle will rock.
When the bough breaks, the cradle will fall
And down will come baby, cradle and all.

There are numerous issues with this nursery rhyme that would shock even the most hardened social worker. Firstly, the baby is left outside in a storm. Secondly, the parents have made the rather bizarre decision to house the baby at the top of a tree. Thirdly, the baby falls. How far, we don't know, but any baby falling from height is normally a bad thing.

Doctor Foster

Doctor Foster
Went to Gloucester
In a shower of rain
He stepped in a puddle
Right up to his middle
And never went there again.

This poor old man has probably seen the most gruesome medical ailments in his time, yet is so traumatised after stepping into what he thought was a shallow puddle only to find himself waist-deep in freezing muddy water that he never goes near Gloucester again. Mind you, I don't blame him.

Hey, Diddle Diddle

Hey, diddle diddle
The cat and the fiddle
The cow jumped over the moon
The little dog laughed to see such fun
And the dish ran away with the spoon.

This rhyme is messed up on a whole number of levels. I can only assume the person who wrote this was high at the time. Where did the dish and spoon go? Behind the bike sheds, I bet. Sickos.

The Grand Old Duke of York

Oh, the grand old Duke of York
He had ten thousand men
He marched them up to the top of the hill
And he marched them down again.

And when they were up they were up
And when they were down they were down
And when they were only halfway up
They were neither up nor down.

This one guy led ten thousand soldiers up to the top of a hill, and down again. I have it on good authority that there was a road that simply went around the hill, but old Yorkie's some kind of sadistic loony. Plus, I bet when they were halfway down he was all like, "Check it out, boys! We're equidistant!" And they're moaning about their blisters and thinking about hacking him to bits.

Ring a Ring o' Roses

Ring a ring o' roses
A pocket full of poses
Atishoo! Atishoo!
We all fall down.

Ashes in the water
Ashes in the sea
We all jump up
With a one, two, three!

Hey, you know that Great Plague that's wiping out millions of people? Let's write a song about how much it sucks, so that people can sing it whilst they die!

Little Jack Horner

Little Jack Horner
Sat in a corner
Eating a Christmas pie.
He put in his thumb
And pulled out a plum
And said "What a good boy am I!"

Whether he's eating *a* Christmas pie, or *his* Christmas pie, the little scrote shouldn't just stick his thumb in it. For one, he could burn himself; and, for another, it's just bad manners. Pick up a fork, you idiot.

Simple Simon

Simple Simon met a pieman going to the fair;
Said Simple Simon to the pieman "Let me taste your ware"
Said the pieman to Simple Simon "Show me first your penny"
Said Simple Simon to the pieman "Sir, I have not any!"

What, you want to taste my pie? Got any cash? Then shove off.

There Was A Crooked Man

There was a crooked man
Who walked a crooked mile
He found a crooked sixpence
Against a crooked stile
He bought a crooked cat
Who caught a crooked mouse
And they all lived together
In a little crooked house.

This man has to walk a mile for some reason. Not only that, he lives in a structurally unsound house with an equally as crooked pet. What did this guy do in his youth that left him so messed up?! Drugs, that's what. Say no, kids. You'll end up with a wonky cat and 6p.

Little Miss Muffet

Little Miss Muffet
Sat on a tuffet
Eating her curds and whey.
Along came a spider
Who sat down beside her
And frightened Miss Muffet away.

The only thing worse than having to eat curds and whey is having a big-ass spider land right next to you as you undoubtedly dry retch all over your tuffet. I heard a rumour she topped herself shortly afterwards. Seriously.

40 NUGGETS OF ADVICE, WISDOM and GENERAL TITBITS

In no particular order…

1. Celebrating the fact your mrs is pregnant is not a valid reason for farting wildly.

2. It is acceptable to run down hospital corridors after the birth of your child looking like you've just scored the winning goal in the World Cup Final.

3. Sliding on your knees, however, is frowned upon; as are Klinsmann dives.

4. It is not acceptable (although funny) to cry out upon the crowning of your child during labour, "What did you *EAT*?!"

5. It is also unacceptable to draw attention to the fact that your partner has squeezed out a poo during labour, despite how incredibly gross it is.

6. Again, it is unacceptable to swaddle the aforementioned stool and pretend it is your baby.

7. Just because her boobs are huge does not mean you have an open invitation to fondle them at every opportunity.

8. If your mrs has just discovered she's pregnant and still has some tests left, it's OK for you to take a test yourself, just to be sure you're not pregnant too.

9. 'Yes' is not an appropriate answer to the question "Is she skinnier than me?"

10. It is unlikely to end well if tell your partner that her stretch marks look like a road map of the UK.

11. However, convincing her they look like tiger stripes might make her feel pretty cool.

12. If your mrs tells you she's having 'a show', don't be fooled into thinking that this involves a stage, actors or pyrotechnics: far from it.

13. During pregnancy, when people ask you if you know what you're having, it's always fun to cross your fingers and say "I'm hoping for a puppy."

14. Pregnant women may bite; approach with caution.

15. When your mrs is on an emotional rollercoaster, please keep your arms and legs inside the vehicle at all times.

16. If your partner eats like a horse, it is ill advised to highlight this by offering her food on a flat palm.

17. Remember, when she is at her most hormonal, it could be worse: you could have *two* pregnant wives. That's why they invented monogamy.

18. When your partner boasts that she has a 'glow', don't burst her bubble by telling her that it's probably sweat produced after she just tried to haul herself off the settee.

19. Watching a one-month old baby peeing on his own face is probably one of the funniest experiences ever.

20. Doing yoga exercises with your partner is remarkably like an extended version of foreplay, only fully clothed and more fun.

21. Be prepared to hear 'I'm carrying your baby' as an excuse for her not doing something. It'll happen. A lot.

22. Your partner's breathing will get heavier during pregnancy, like listening to Darth Vader with nasal congestion.

23. Even though her bum *does* look big in that, officially, it does *not* look big in that.

24. Be prepared; your mrs blames you, and only you, for all pain or discomfort she feels during pregnancy, despite forgetting that it was somewhat of a team effort to get there.

25. Not just the pain; everything will be your fault, and will somehow relate to you fertilising her.

26. You can say very little to comfort her when she is dreading labour, but don't make things worse by demonstrating the probable size of the newborn with your hands.

27. Nothing is more of a turn-on than a heavily pregnant woman's waddle.

28. A little cup of tea can go a long way.

29. The best things in life are free, and come in small packages. A baby falls into neither of these categories.

30. It is frowned upon to huff gas and air during labour whilst your mrs goes without.

31. It's OK to cry at the birth of your child, but too much sobbing will brand you as a blubbering softie.

32. Don't get too excited when your baby rolls over/crawls/speaks for the first time. Soon enough, you'll be wishing they'd never learnt.

33. Nothing can match the sense of achievement felt upon hearing your baby emit a throaty belch after a marathon half-hour of back patting.

34. It's fine for you and your mrs to cheer the first time your child pees into a potty, but don't expect the same reaction from them if you do it too.

35. Somehow, fatherhood results in a superpower: the ability to have baby poo on your finger and not freak out.

36. Under times of stress or excessive wriggling, poppers are impossible to do up.

37. The face that babies and toddlers pull when squeezing out a poo is really funny, and should be filmed for posterity.

38. Feeding your child strong cheese just to laugh at his revolted expression is not a good party trick, and is probably illegal.

39. Despite similarities, the phrase 'baby shower' has nothing to do with 'raining cats and dogs'.

40. Cabbage leaves in the bra may not relieve mastitis. Instead, it will just smell and make hospital doctors very confused.

ANCIENT CHINESE GENDER CHART

Discovered in a royal tomb in Beijing, this chart is over 700 years old and said to be 90-99% accurate. Using the month you conceived and your partner's lunar age* at the time of conception, work out if you're having a boy or a girl!

Month of Conception

Age	Jan	Feb	Mar	Apr	May	Jun	Jul	Aug	Sep	Oct	Nov	Dec
18	F	M	F	M	M	M	M	M	M	M	M	M
19	M	F	M	F	F	M	M	F	M	M	F	F
20	F	M	F	M	M	M	M	M	M	F	M	M
21	M	F	F	F	F	F	F	F	F	F	F	F
22	F	M	M	F	M	F	F	M	F	F	F	F
23	M	M	M	F	M	M	F	F	F	M	M	F
24	M	F	F	M	M	F	M	F	M	M	F	M
25	F	M	F	M	F	M	F	M	F	M	M	M
26	M	M	M	M	M	F	M	F	F	M	F	F
27	F	F	M	M	F	M	F	F	M	F	M	M
28	M	M	M	F	F	M	F	M	F	F	M	F
29	F	M	F	F	M	F	M	M	F	M	F	F
30	M	M	F	M	F	M	M	M	M	M	M	M
31	M	M	M	M	F	F	M	F	M	F	F	F
32	M	F	F	M	F	M	M	F	M	M	F	M
33	F	M	M	F	F	M	F	M	F	M	M	F
34	M	M	F	F	M	F	M	M	F	M	F	F
35	M	F	M	F	M	F	M	F	M	M	F	M
36	M	F	M	M	M	F	M	M	F	F	F	F
37	F	F	M	F	F	F	M	F	F	M	M	M
38	M	M	F	F	M	F	F	M	F	F	M	F
39	F	F	M	F	F	F	M	F	M	M	F	M
40	M	M	M	F	M	F	M	F	M	F	F	M
41	F	F	M	F	M	M	F	F	M	F	M	F
42	M	F	F	M	M	M	M	M	F	M	F	M
43	F	M	F	F	M	M	M	F	F	F	M	M
44	M	F	F	F	M	F	M	M	F	M	F	M
45	F	M	F	M	F	F	M	F	M	F	M	F

* Lunar age = actual age + 2 years

With thanks to KarenCheng.com.au

GLOSSARY

This might help you out when midwives, your mrs and people you don't even know start spouting jargon which fries your mind.

These are just a few of the thousands around.

A

Afterbirth	All the goo and placenta that comes out after the baby's birth. Not really something to be waited for with bated breath.
Amniocentesis	A test for foetal abnormalities where amniotic fluid is drawn from the sac surrounding the baby. There is a slight risk of miscarriage with this procedure.
Amniotic Fluid	The gooey liquid in the sac surrounding your baby. Not suitable for drinking.
Amniotic Sac	The sac that surrounds the baby. Keep up.
Anterior	Baby is face down (the right way) when it gets squeezed out into this world.
Areola	The dark area around the nipple. You should know this by now. How old are you?

B

Birth Canal The passageway your baby travels down between the uterus and the outside world during delivery. Like a normal canal, without the weeds and ducks.

Birth Plan A list of requests and information for the midwife regarding pain relief, number of people present at the birth, etc.

Birth Stories Where glassy-eyed women talk wistfully about birth, leaving out the bit where they did a poo on the floor.

Blastocyst The stage of embryo development five days after fertilisation.

Bloody Show Blood-tinged vaginal mucous, probably indicating the loss of the mucous plug. Not to be confused with an angry remark about a poor TV programme.

Braxton-Hicks Practice contractions. Normally not painful, but this doesn't mean you can be nonchalant whilst your mrs freaks out.

Breastfeeding Allowing women to get their boobs out in public since 1901.

Breech When the baby is bum down

instead of head down. Occurs
in fewer than 5% of births.

C

Caesarean	When they get the baby out through another hole instead of the pre-made one. You know the rest.
Cervix	The grand entrance to the uterus; opens to 10cm during birth.
Chorionic Villus Sampling (CVS)	Another test for birth defects, which can be done earlier than the amniocentesis (between 9 and 11 weeks).
Colostrum	A thin white liquid rich in antibodies that often leaks out of your partner's milkers in the last few weeks of pregnancy.
Conception	When the sperm penetrates the egg, you old dog you.
Constipation	You know what this is; I just put it in 'cos it's funny.
Contraception	The thing you didn't use which got your mrs pregnant in the first place.
Couvade	Where men experience the physical symptoms and pains associated with pregnancy. Also known as 'being a big girl'.
Craving	What your mrs uses as an excuse for gorging herself on delicious food.

Crowning

When your baby's head is
pushing through the cervix.
Not really very nice to watch.

D

Dilation

The opening of your partner's
cervix during delivery.

Discharge

White mucous secretions from
the vagina. So gross it's hard
to put into words.

Doppler

A device which allows you to
listen to the foetal heartbeat.

Doula

A woman who helps a family
through childbirth. Also, my
DJ name.

E

Eclampsia

High blood pressure caused
by pregnancy. Can be very
dangerous to mother and
baby.

Effacement

The thinning of the cervix in
preparation for birth.

Elective
Caesarean

When a C-Section is
specifically requested.

Embryo

What your baby is for the first
eight weeks from conception.

Endometrium

The lining of the uterus that is
usually released during
periods, along with sporadic
bouts of irrational anger.

Engaged

When the baby's head is well
and truly buried in your mrs'

	pelvis, usually in the last month of pregnancy.
Epidural	A common form of pain relief during pregnancy, where anaesthetic is administered into the space near the spinal cord.
Episiotomy	Where the midwives cut your partner's perineum to widen the opening.

F

Face Presentation	An uncommon delivery presentation when the baby is positioned in such a way that it is looking down the birth canal. I imagine a pair of glowing eyes at the cervix…
First Trimester	The first 12 weeks of pregnancy.
Foetus	Your baby from eight weeks of pregnancy until delivery.
Folic Acid	Essential to reduce the risk of certain birth defects, such as spina bifida.
Forceps	A pair of tongs (slightly different from those you use to cook a BBQ) that helps guide the baby out during delivery.
Fundal Height	The measurement taken from the top of the pubic bone to the top of the uterus; used to assess baby growth and

development.

G

Gestation — The nine months in which your baby cooks in the oven. Not literally, of course.

Gestational Diabetes — A condition during pregnancy where the mother cannot produce enough insulin to break sugars down into energy.

German Measles — Also known as Rubella, an illness which – in pregnant women – can result in birth defects. Has absolutely nothing to do with Germans.

GYN — An abbreviation for gynaecologist (otherwise known as someone who looks at front bottoms for a living).

H

Haemorrhage — Excessive bleeding.

Haemorrhoid — Also known as piles; enlarged veins in the anus or rectum, common in pregnancy or after childbirth. Also very gross.

HCG — Human Chorionic Gonadotrophin: the hormone that pregnancy tests look out for.

Home Birth — When you have the birth at home. Did you really need to look this one up?

Hypnobirthing	A technique for installing positive thinking in the mother to prepare them for birth.

I

Incontinence	When she wees herself without meaning to. Snigger.
Implantation	When the embryo attaches itself to the lining of the uterus.
In Utero	The posh way of saying 'in the uterus'.
Iron Deficiency	Also known as anaemia, when the iron content of the blood is very low, leading to tiredness.

J

Jaundice	A common condition in newborns where the liver cannot process excess red blood cells. Makes the skin slightly yellow.

K

Kegel Exercises	Pelvic floor exercises to help strengthen the various muscles used during delivery.

L

Lamaze	A childbirth preparation

method, focussing on
relaxation and breathing
techniques.

Lanugo	A fine hair that covers the foetus through most of pregnancy. Not to be confused with pubic hair, or fur.
Linea Nigra	A dark brown line that sometimes appears from the belly button down to the pubic bone.

M

Malpresentation	Where the baby is not head down before delivery. See Breech and Face Presentation.
Mask of Pregnancy	Brown pigmentation on the cheeks and forehead of a pregnant woman.
Meconium	Your baby's first poo; usually greeny black and always very gross. Sometimes done whilst still in the womb.
Morning Sickness	Nausea which is not limited to the morning. How misleading.
Mucous Plug	The gooey plug that blocks the cervix during pregnancy. See *Bloody Show*.

N

Neonatal	The first four weeks of a

	baby's life. Nothing to do with 'The Matrix', unfortunately.
Nesting	The urge a woman gets to clean, nearing the end of her pregnancy. More than usual, of course.
NICU	Neonatal Intensive Care Unit.
Nuchal Translucency Test	A scan to help identify the risk of Down's Syndrome by measuring the amount of fluid behind the neck of the foetus.
Nonuplets	Nine babies at once. Nine. Bordering on the ridiculous.

O

Obstetrician	A doctor who specialises in pregnancy and childbirth.
OB/GYN	The abbreviation for a doctor who specialises in the female reproductive system and the delivery of babies.
Oxytocin	The hormone secreted by the pituitary gland that stimulates contractions.

P

Perineum	The tissue between the vagina and anus. Why did you make me write that?
Pica	A condition whereby the woman craves inedible things, like coal or dirt. Very weird.
Placenta	The fleshy tissue that

	nourishes the foetus and removes waste products.
Placenta Previa	A low-lying placenta, often obstructing the opening of the uterus. Sounds like a model of car.
Preeclampsia	A dangerous condition characterised by high blood pressure and excessive swelling.
Premature Labour	Labour beginning before the 37th week of pregnancy.
Preterm	Babies born before the 37th week of pregnancy.
Pubic Symphysis	The joint between the pelvic bones at the front (known as the pubis).

Q

Quattrodecaplets	A multiple birth consisting of 14 babies. Now *that* is just insane.
Quindecaplets	Fifteen babies. Now you're just being stupid.

R

Ripening	The softening and thinning of the cervix as it prepares for delivery of the foetus. Absolutely nothing to do with juicy apples.
Rubella	See *German Measles*.

S

Sciatica	Pain in the lower back, bottom and legs, caused by pressure on the Sciatic nerve.
SPD	Symphis Pubis Dysfunction. Where the pelvic joints relax too much, causing pain when moving.
Spina Bifida	A birth defect characterised by the incomplete formation of the foetus' backbone.
Spotting	Light bleeding, most common during the first trimester.
SIDS	Sudden Infant Death Syndrome.
Sonogram	The ultrasound scan.
Sperm	What you produced to kick all this off, you great stallion.

T

Term	The full 40 week pregnancy.
Tilted Uterus	Where the top of the uterus is tilted towards the back of the body, instead of towards the front.
Toxoplasmosis	A disease that can cause harm to the foetus. Often found in raw meat and cat poo.
Transverse	Where the baby is lying horizontally in the uterus.
Trimester	A 12-week period.

U

Umbilical Cord   The tube that carries oxygen
                       and nutrients to the foetus
                       from the placenta.

Uterine Fibroids   Harmless growths on the wall
                       of the uterus.

Uterine Rupture   A tear in the wall of the uterus
                       that can be life-threatening to
                       mother and baby.

V

Vagina   Don't make me spell it out for
                       you.

Vernix Caseosa   The white, cheesy goo that
                       covers your foetus during the
                       final stages of pregnancy to
                       keep it warm and slick.

W

Water Retention   Also known as Oedema. The
                       swelling of soft tissues due to
                       excessive fluid.

X

X-ray   You know what an X-ray is.
                       Stop being daft.

Y

"Y?!"   The abbreviated screams of
                       an anguished man, or a
                       woman in labour.

Z

Zygote	The cell that is the result of fertilisation.
Zzz...	Sleep. Something which you won't be getting much of now.

USEFUL LINKS

A few links for more info on being a dad, and the support you can get. Also, my blog, which is hilarious.

Goodbye, Pert Breasts: The Blog
http://www.goodbyepertbreasts.com
My blog. Read about things that will make you giggle and cause a little bit of pee to come out.

The Fatherhood Institute
http://www.fatherhoodinstitute.org/
The UK's fatherhood think tank, and a great information source.

Dads UK
http://www.dads-uk.co.uk
A news and information site about fathers' rights.

Dad.info
http://www.dad.info
As the name suggests, info about and for dads.

Only Dads
http://www.onlydads.org
Support and advice for single fathers.

THE END...NOT

You'll see what I've done there. I've skilfully taken the two words that end many a book, and added the sarcasm of a stroppy teenager. I went to all this trouble to signify that this is not the end, but just the beginning of fatherhood, and being the best dad you can be.

But although you're at the start of a long journey, you shouldn't fear: it's an exciting path, and one full of milestones – when your baby rolls over, walks, goes to school, graduates from university, gets arrested - to name but a few. Between these milestones runs a road that will give you highs, lows, anger and sadness; but you'll love every minute of it, because you're a father now, and your little boy or girl has suddenly become the most important thing in your life – shunting any other issues you have going on to the side and into perspective, like a fat person ploughing through a crowd at a bakery to get a free sample of chocolate cake.

Take a minute – in private, to avoid strange looks – to give yourself a pat on the back, or a high five; which is, in essence, simply a single clap. Look how far you've come already: nine months of pain, discomfort and frustration – and no, I'm not talking about your mrs. You've had to adapt to being a father, and in doing so you've probably become a better partner as well. Whilst perhaps not evident as she swiped at your face during labour, your significant other would have been immensely grateful for every foot rub you gave, every cup of tea you made, every time you went out to the shops to buy nothing but ultra-absorbent panty-liners, risking your hard-earned masculinity in the process. Of course, sometimes these helpful acts were carried out begrudgingly; it would only be in a perfect world or on a 1950's advert where you would be a permanently doting partner, grinning emptily in glorious Technicolor like a maniac as your mrs cries incessantly for no reason. But we don't live in a perfect world, and until someone invents a way to get the first sheet of toilet paper off the roll without tearing the whole thing to shreds, I won't believe that we are.

There will have been times when you were frustrated, annoyed, exhausted – and, probably, a bit scared. You may still feel these feelings, and this is completely normal. But gaze into your baby's eyes, and look at your own reflection; unless they're asleep, in which case prying his or her eyelids open would be a bad move and heavily frowned upon. Instead, just look at your child, at its face, its little fingers, its little chest moving up and down with each breath, and ask yourself: Would I give anything to make them happy and keep them safe?

I think I know what your answer is: and you're going to be just fine.

It's strange, but when I was really young I always used to admire my dad for the way he made buttering toast look so easy. No-one could butter toast as well as my dad. And I guess that's the kind of admiration that I would like to prompt in Noah, as well as Isaac: not just the big things, like having respect because I'm a good father, or whatever - but an unspoken admiration and pride for the little things, the day-to-day things that you do now because you're a parent, and that's what parents do. If you've had the patience with me to reach the end of this book, then I reckon you probably care enough to want the same.

This, my friend, is where we part ways. I'll perhaps see you in some baby/infant playgroup; I'll be the one knee-deep in toddlers, looking stressed, getting poo on my thumb and quietly craving a good sit down. Then again, I've just described every parent in the entire history of the world.

You know full well by now, if your mrs has sprogged a little 'un, that parenthood can be tough, draining and stressful; but it's also pretty much the best thing in the world. You could score in the Champions League Final, or climb Everest, and still not feel the exhilaration you experience when you hold your child for the first time.

There's a long way to go yet; this is just the beginning. We've got the terrible twos to look forward to, the stress of choosing a school, parents' evening, the spotty adolescent moodiness...but hey, look on the bright side: only eighteen more years until they leave home.

THE BEGINNING.

4277391R00152

Printed in Great Britain
by Amazon.co.uk, Ltd.,
Marston Gate.